PRAISE FOR A LIFE IN STITCHES

"Insightfully genius, A Life in Stitches makes me grateful that Rachael Herron put down her needles long enough to pick up a pen."

—Josh Kilmer-Purcell, *New York Times* bestselling author of *The Bucolic Plague*

"Herron breaks the heart and knits it back together again with stories of how knitting bound her with family, friend, and lovers. This book is a beautiful example of how to build a life, and a memoir, one stitch at a time."

– Sue Cauhape

"A must-read for all, knitters and non. Then buy it for your girlfriends and mom and sister and your brother who knits, too. Rachael Herron just gets it."

– *True/Stories Review*

ALSO BY RACHAEL HERRON

Standalone Novels:

The Ones Who Matter Most

Splinters of Light

Pack Up the Moon

Stolen Things (as R.H. Herron)

Hush Little Baby (as R.H. Herron)

The Darling Bay Novels:

The Darling Songbirds

The Songbird's Call

The Songbird Sisters

The Ballard Brothers of Darling Bay:

On the Market

Build it Strong

Rock the Boat

The Firefighters of Darling Bay:

Blaze

Burn

Flame

Heat

Cypress Hollow Novels:

Abigail's Shop

Lucy's Kiss

Naomi's Wish

Cora's Heart

Fiona's Flame

Eliza's Home

Memoir:

A Life in Stitches: Knitting My Way through Love, Loss, and Laughter - Tenth Anniversary Edition

Nonfiction:

Fast-Draft Your Memoir: Write Your Life Story in 45 Hours

Fast-Draft Your Memoir: The Workbook

Letters to New Authors: 29 Encouraging Letters to Your Inner Writer

A LIFE IN STITCHES

KNITTING MY WAY THROUGH LOVE, LOSS, AND LAUGHTER

RACHAEL HERRON

TENTH ANNIVERSARY EDITION

CONTENTS

ISBN: 978-1-940785-61-5

HGA Publishing

FOREWORD

By Clara Parkes

Thanks to knitting and a little eucalyptus-spotted piece of land in Oakland, California, I knew Rachael Herron long before I actually knew her. In the spring of 1991, I could be found on most Saturday nights sprawled on one of the dandelion-colored couches in the living room of Orchard Meadow Hall at Mills College. I was joined by my friends Emily Jane, Hilair, and Jenny for what we called—in a very smug, antiestablishment tone—the Saturday night crafters.

Emily Jane was perpetually in the process of turning the heel on a sock that never, to my knowledge, got finished. Hilair embroidered botanical prints of her own design, whereas Jenny dutifully slogged away on a giant pink acrylic afghan that she'd been crocheting for her grandmother since high school. And I rowed back and forth on an equally endless blue stockinette sweater whose finished pieces still await their seaming today—I'm just waiting for cropped, dolman-sleeved boatnecks to come back in style. Then, as now, I knit for the doing.

Mills was proudly and defiantly a women's college. The previous year the students had barricaded themselves in the administrative offices to protest the board of directors' decision to open up the college to men. (The board reversed its decision.) And, while some dorms were known to be a little more friendly to the hope chest–coveting crowd that dated the UC Berkeley guys named Dave, I was in the dorm closest to the athletics, theater, and music departments—which made it a hybrid hotbed of performance artists and boisterous crew jocks. I was neither, but I found the blend so comforting that I stayed in the same dorm, in the same hallway even, my entire time at Mills.

Feminism was in its second wave, a charged yet increasingly amorphous concept that people took turns claiming and then rejecting depending on the circumstances. We wrote papers condemning the male-dominated patriarchy, we marched to reclaim our power, and we tried to figure out how we wanted these principles to play out in our own lives. We spread the word "women" like butter on our toast every morning, and we were quick to correct anyone who dared call us "girls."

By the spring of 1991, I was a senior facing the last few months of academic cosseting before being pushed back out into the real world. I had absolutely no clue how I was going to stay afloat; I just kept hoping I'd find a job description that read: "Dreamer wanted. Must speak fluent French and have excellent parallel-parking abilities."

I took comfort in spending as much time with my friends as possible, knowing that no matter how hard we tried, things would never be the same after we walked across that stage with our diplomas. My friends and I all worked as receptionists in our dorm, and we had a tradition of keeping one another company on the late Saturday night shift. (This was just before the internet had taken hold, way back when people relied on the physical presence of others for company.) Somehow it took us three and a half years to discover that we all knew how to make things with our hands, and it was a welcome, surprising revelation. Craft was such a secret, private part of our identities that nobody had ever brought it up, or if we had, clearly nobody was paying attention.

We decided to do something radical with our Saturday nights. Hilair grabbed her embroidery, I my blue sweater, Jenny the giant pink afghan, and Emily Jane the sock. We took up residence in the living room, where we proudly, loudly, and quite probably obnoxiously announced our crafty inclination to any soul who passed us by.

We were honor students, members of the student government, recipients of awards and grants and scholarships. We were being pushed to become ball-busting CEOs, to break gender stereotypes and shatter that glass ceiling once and for all—or to create parallel worlds in which any ceiling was of our own creation. But once every weekend, we found a time and place for something much slower and more satisfying.

Knitting hadn't yet reclaimed the positive image it has today in popular culture. For us, knitting in the dorm living room on a Saturday night was tantamount to donning a corset and churning butter by the fire before blowing out the candles and saying, "Good night, John-Boy." Only in baggy T-shirts and leggings.

And yet, as with all things, our revolution soon drew to a close. We graduated and moved on. And despite our best attempts, it *wasn't* the same ever again.

I never did find that full-time French-speaking, parallel-parking dreamer job. Nor did I become a ball-busting CEO. I worked with words, bouncing from field to field and job to job. Knitting never stopped yipping at my heels, though. In 2000, I finally heeded the call and launched my online knitting magazine, *Knitter's Review*. I quickly found myself once again surrounded by women (and men) doing beautiful things with yarn, needles, and their hands. For the first time since those Saturday nights on the dandelion-colored couch, I was knitting in the company of others. It felt welcome and familiar.

And the others? Emily Jane still knits, and Hilair still embroiders when the urge strikes. We lost Jenny in a car accident in 2004, but I'd like to think she's up there in the clouds, still working away on that big pink afghan.

Meanwhile, just six years after my blue sweater and I departed from the Mills campus, a young MFA student named Rachael Herron arrived. There, in the same eucalyptus-shaded buildings, she studied English and creative writing, she published a literary magazine, and she knit. A lot.

She started blogging about knitting at Yarnagogo.com, and, unbeknownst to me, she was reading my *Knitter's Review*. We spent many years like this in our parallel orbits, knowing and liking one another without ever actually meeting. When we finally did meet, the friendship was sealed.

For me, the essays in this book provide deeper detail and higher contrast to a painting I'd begun outlining in my head years ago. They show how knitting can infuse itself in a far broader, deeper human experience. They're a pleasure to read—a laugh, a surprise, a nod of understanding—and I know you'll enjoy them.

INTRODUCTION

Welcome to the tenth anniversary edition of this book! If you read the first edition of this and want to read only the new stuff, I'll cut to the chase and tell you it's at the end. But even if you've read this before, it might stand up to a reread. I'm a better writer than I was ten years ago, so I took some time to go back through these essays and make them tighter and stronger. I've removed some of the pilling and I've darned the weak spots. Back when this was released, it was my third published book but now I've written and published more than two dozen. I'm a full-time writer—I wasn't when this was first written. My life looks different now, and it's about to get *really* different, as at the time of this writing, we're just weeks away from moving around the world to New Zealand.

Time is tricky, isn't it? It feels like only a few moments have passed since the first edition came out, but then again, how do I measure time?

People measure their lives by many things. Some measure their days by how many races they've run. Some mark turning points by the songs they've loved. T. S. Eliot's Prufrock "measured out his life in coffee spoons," and others, when attaching meaning to incidents, look at when the children came, or when their parents got sick, or which house they were living in at the time.

My life can be measured in lengths of yarn: what kind of fiber I held, at what time. Always, as far back as I can remember, I've had a knitting project somewhere close by, and no matter what emotion I'm feeling, I put some of it into the stitches I make. Grief translates into tighter stitches more likely to stand up to heavy wear, while happiness makes my knitting a looser gauge. It's more likely to pill later, but I think pills show character. Luckily, more of my knitting is the happy, pilly kind.

I'm a memoirist with a shabby memory. Luckily, I have a mnemonic system: I fold and stack my knitted sweaters in two tall white bookcases, and as I run my eye down the colors, I can remember where I was when I made each sweater. That orange sweater I made with yarn I carried home from Belgium—ten skeins I stuffed into an already overstuffed suitcase—only to find that the exact yarn was available at my local yarn store in Oakland. The fiber still felt exotic to knit, and as I worked the cables, I remembered the way the afternoon light fell into a tree-lined square as I sat by myself eating frites, drinking a dark amber Belgian beer. The green one is made from heavy cashmere bought during my first trip to New York City, when I was overcome by the city's electric pulse, and its gold buttons are from a trip to Venice, found in a button display discovered during a quick glance into a hardware shop. It was warm and muggy in both cities, and the cashmere weighs heavy, like a thick blanket on my shoulders.

And those buttons, there, are Edwardian, from the late 1800s. They cost more than the yarn for two sweaters, and I think of them as my button folly. But they remind me of my Edwardian diamond engagement ring, and of my mother's engagement ring crafted in the same time period. When I touch the buttons, I see her emerald ring in my mind's eye, and I'm pleased.

I'm sure I'd still be knitting, still attaching memories to wool and silk and alpaca, even if the internet revolution hadn't changed knitting as much as it did, but I'm grateful that I was around at the beginning of it all. For so many years, I knitted alone. I was positive I was the only twenty-something doing it, and the knitting patterns sold at the chain craft stores didn't dissuade me of this notion. I could take my pick of afghan and teddy bear patterns, but it was hard to find fashionable, wearable patterns on the spinner racks next to the puff paint aisle.

Then I stumbled upon something called a blog. I loved Carolyn's website, called Dangerous Chunky, even though I didn't understand it. The information on it changed daily! She wrote about knitting, and from her voice, she sounded a lot like *me*: Young. Urban. Trying to be creative with the tools we loved. I had to know more. I dove headfirst into the rapidly growing knitting community, and I suppose I haven't come up for air since.

Throughout the years, I've learned that everyone thinks stockinette is ideal for car rides. Most think socks are appropriate for planes, since you don't have to elbow your neighbor overly much. I've discovered that the Sweater

Curse is just a myth, but it's one that knitters don't fool around with. I've realized that nowhere is too far to go for the yarn of your dreams, but sometimes it's best to stay home and make your own. Most of all, I've learned that knitters aren't all the same. There are perfectionist knitters, and knitters who can't be bothered to learn more than one cast-on (like me). There are delighted knitters and grumpy ones, tall ones and short ones, but knitters, overall, are the nicest people in the world, and I mean that with all my heart. Just recently, I asked MaryEllen on Ravelry (who didn't know me from Adam) to mail her hot-water bottle and its cozy, which she'd made from my pattern, to New York for a photo shoot, because I was lame and didn't own one myself. And she *did*. Graciously. The very same day she was asked. She did it because another knitter asked her to, plain and simple, and she exemplifies the generosity of knitters everywhere.

And now, my life cannot only be measured by *things*, the sweaters I've made, but by the people who sat near me (either literally or virtually) while I knitted, the people who helped when I couldn't figure out a particular join, the people who've become my friends. This idea warms me, and I pull it around me like my favorite sweater (which I'll tell you about in this book).

Enjoy. And then, perhaps, share this book with your best knitting friend, and feel grateful, as I do, that we're part of the most wonderful community in the world.

CASTING ON

*I*never was a Daddy's girl. I loved my father, but I
didn't understand him. With three girls and a
wife, he was the only guy in an all-girl household. Even our
cats were female. I felt like my father came from a different
planet. He said things a little too loudly, did things a little
too quickly, and even the way he smelled of oil and pipe
tobacco seemed strange and somehow foreign, as if he
were a beloved visitor, one to be humored and then left
alone to his customs.

An aspiring entrepreneur, he always believed a million-
dollar idea was just around the corner. He loved cruising
neighborhoods in our VW van, hitting the brakes so hard
when he saw garage sale signs that we would fly forward
and land in a pile on the shag carpeting. He'd search each
sale, looking for his next big find that would surely hurtle
him into wealth: a button-making machine (who doesn't
want personalized buttons?), a dehydrator (turkey jerky's
the new thing!). We loved garage sale hunting, too, coming
home with broken Barbies and board games with missing

pieces, not caring that we'd have to use Monopoly pieces to play Candy Land.

One particular Saturday morning, while Dad was trawling for business opportunities in piles of other people's crap, I struck the yarn mother lode. There it was, in all its blueness: a pile of 100 percent acrylic. I'd never seen yarn that color; it was so blue it looked electrically charged. It pulsed at me from the box sitting in the dry, brown grass. It was the most thrilling color I'd ever seen.

My meager allowance already spent earlier in the morning on candy, I begged my father to buy it for me. There were eight balls of lint-covered toxic blue yarn in the box, marked at a quarter each. It was the bargain of the century. He had to understand that.

"Can you get 'em down to a nickel each?" he said while looking at a rusted saw.

I was eleven. I would rather *die* than haggle.

"Please?"

"Why do you need it? You always knit with Mom's yarn anyway. She's still got lots of leftovers, right?"

"But this would make a whole sweater."

He didn't seem to hear me. He poked at something that looked like a saddle.

Then it hit me. I knew what I needed to do to convince him. "I'm going to make sweaters and sell them." I chickened out at the last minute and added a qualifying "I think." I wasn't sure I'd actually end up wanting to knit for money, but how much did it hurt to let him think I did? And maybe it *would* be fun and profitable.

One thing about my father: speculate about an interesting money-making venture that involves a ship and a pirate and sharks circling below with gold coins in their teeth, and he'll be first in line to walk the plank.

He handed me two dollars.

At home, I cast on with wild abandon, not knowing I would soon be knitting into a black hole of a serious lack of knowledge. I didn't do a gauge swatch—I didn't even know what one was. I'd never followed a pattern in my life, and I'd be starting with one from the fifties that I'd found in my mother's cedar chest. I didn't think it looked *too* dated—a simple raglan with no shaping and crew neck collar. I chose size medium arbitrarily, because it didn't cross my mind that it was possible to measure myself and compare those measurements to those on the page.

I just wanted to knit a sweater. Just as I'd had the urge to teach myself stenography and drawing from books (I'd failed, by the way—I'd never make my living in the courtroom by either taking notes or sketching tense scenes), I was following an autodidactic impulse to teach myself how to knit a whole sweater, using the pattern as my tutor. The fabric would fly off my needles, I knew it. I was ready.

I flipped on my clock radio. Duran Duran. Perfect. I curled up on my bed. I had no clue what I was getting myself into. I steamed ahead, happily looking forward to the day I could wear my sweater to school and wow my sixth-grade peers.

Dad came up the stairs and popped his head in to see how my new capitalistic venture was going. I shooed him out. No time to talk.

Not liking the idea of knitting a whole back or a whole front, I cast on for the flat-knitted sleeves first. Ribbing. I knew how to do this, just knits and purls. Easy.

Then, suddenly, the instructions told me to switch to stockinette and increase every five rows. I understood stockinette, but how would I increase? I turned the pages of the brittle leaflet with increasing panic. I could have, of course, gone downstairs and asked my mother, but this was *my* project, and if she picked it up and started doing things with it, it would become partly hers, less mine. I didn't want to give up any part of it, and, more than that, I wanted to have bragging rights by the end: "I did this all by myself. No one helped me." I would stand proud when I said it, wearing electric blue.

Increasing, increasing. Here it was. "Increase by making one," it said. That was all it said. Were they serious? I knew how to cast on; was it like that? I had a feeling I was close, but I couldn't make it work. Finally, I ended up just looping the yarn over the needle and hoping for the best.

My sister Christy climbed the steps to my room and asked if I wanted to go play on the stilts Dad was helping her make.

I shook my head. "Nope. Knitting a sweater."

"But it's fun. Dad said he'll make you a pair of stilts too. He wants to sell them if they work out. Will you be done soon?"

"Probably."

Six months later, I was still dragging that blue yarn around. Kids at school teased me when it trailed out of my backpack. The electric color that had looked so mod, so exciting, at the yard sale now just looked like something a grandmother would crochet for a tissue-box cover.

Dad watched my hands as I stubbornly knitted while we watched TV.

"So, you're pretty fast, huh?"

"Yep," I said. At night, I liked to sit in our living room and use the window glass as a mirror, watching my hands flash. Seen in reverse, it made them look like someone else's hands, not attached to my body. The fingers went so quickly, moved so nimbly. I was vain about the way I knitted. "I'm *very* fast."

"How much can you get for a sweater?"

I shrugged.

"But you think you can really make money doing that?" he asked.

"How's the bumper-sticker business?"

We grimaced at each other and went back to watching *M.A.S.H.*

Of course, it turned out to be the ugliest sweater in creation. For starters, I made a huge error with the neckline. When it said to bind off loosely, I didn't think it was necessary. I didn't want my stitches to be saggy—the garment already looked wonky enough. And I was in a blazing hurry. So I sewed it up using an unholy combination of backstitch and double crochet, thinking, *Just these last final steps of binding off, and the sweater will be done!* I'd pull it over my head, my doubts would go away, and though it looked pretty strange on my lap, I was sure it would look great on.

I bound off. I wove the end in so completely, so thoroughly, that it was completely hidden. I was *good*.

Then I slowly stood up.

I tried to pull it over my face.

It was impossible.

I hadn't bound off loosely enough. After all those

months of work, I couldn't get my head through the neck hole. And I couldn't even find where I'd so carefully woven in the end to undo it.

I panicked and pulled harder. I managed to get the sweater over my head—the skin on my face was nearly scraped off from the rough acrylic, but it was on. My mother stifled her gasp when she saw me and said weakly, "Well done." My sisters laughed and laughed.

To make matters worse, I dropped a few stitches right at the bust line, and somehow I thought it would be okay to sew them closed with white thread, thinking it would be invisible from the front. I was wrong. An early-developing eleven-year-old girl needs absolutely no help drawing attention to her bust. The sleeves were one step away from lace and barely stayed together with all the yarn-overs. And the whole thing was three sizes too big for me.

I was deathly nervous to show it to my father. He'd had even higher hopes than I had, and I'd screwed it up. I was an entrepreneurial-knitting failure. Whatever fantasy I'd entertained to make money by knitting died a rapid death in front of the mirror. I made my way into Dad's hobby room, where he was whittling wood into crib toys, a pipe clenched between his teeth, wood-shavings at his feet. My scratched face blazed.

"So that's your prototype?" he asked.

I tugged at the collar, which was so tight it made breathing difficult. "I don't think I'm going to make sweaters for money."

He shrugged. "It's a good color on you."

I looked at him in surprise. "You're not mad?"

"About what? You finished it." He nodded and pulled on

his pipe. "I think that's great. Hey, what do you think about a mobile carwash business?"

I never wore the sweater once I finally got it back off, taking another layer of my face with it. I was already unpopular enough with my glasses and braces and tendency to do things like knit—I didn't want to make things worse with the kids at school. But I had finished my first sweater. It didn't make me cool. And knitting wouldn't make me money.

But my dad, who'd started and scrapped at least four new businesses since the start of that year, thought it was pretty neat. I could see in his eyes that he believed I'd done something great, just because I finished it. And I thought it was pretty great too: I'd learned how to follow a pattern and how to create a whole garment, using simple sticks and string. I understood, finally, his excitement about starting things and the satisfaction that could be gained from carrying them through to completion, even when they were obvious disasters. Because when I looked at my awful sweater, the first thing I thought was, *Oh, crap.* The second thing I thought was, *How can I make the next one better?*

Hope always came right behind disaster in my dad's world—if the poor man's gas grill cobbled together from an old hibachi and a propane tank didn't work, then it just meant that he'd have to come up with the next big million-dollar idea. And the idea would come. It always did.

We both sat in the living room that night watching *M.A.S.H.* with unseeing eyes. I wondered if it would be hard to knit slippers, and if there might possibly be a market for them. They'd be faster to knit than sweaters, that was sure. He was probably plotting something that involved selling tooled leather at the flea market. Like father, like daughter. And that was all right by me.

*T*en Years Later
In this new edition, in some (but not all) of the chapters, I'll give you a little update on what's happened since I wrote the essay. Here, I want to go on record as saying that my father is *really* proud that in 2016, I was able to quit my day job and become a full-time writer. I'm my own boss, literally living the entrepreneurial dream. Staying at home to write while being able to pay the bills with money I make from words that come out of my head? Well, it's the best thing ever, even better than I ever dreamed it would be. My dad's a writer, just like my mother was, so I owe them both a debt of gratitude. This writing life is amazing. Thanks, Dad.

SLIP KNOT

*W*hen I was twelve, my father, who'd always had the feet of a wanderer, got a job overseas. My family moved from California to a tiny island in the middle of the Western Pacific. Saipan, just twelve miles long by three miles wide, was a star in the Northern Mariana constellation, and from our living room we looked over the lagoon and out into the dark blue waters of the deepest trench in the world. While we lived in this paradise, I was trying to figure out how to grow up.

We'd packed our suitcases full of essentials—soap, cutlery, plates—and shipped everything else. We lived on the island for months before the boat delivered our other precious belongings: books, and records, and games. But I'd made a crucial mistake when packing. At twelve, I wasn't very good at planning for the future. When told I could ship my own box, I'd filled it with books, blank journals, construction paper, and crayons. Then, at the last minute, still wobbling on the fence-rail between childhood and adolescence, I'd added my beloved stuffed cat. Between the books and the plush toy, my yarn didn't fit, so I left it behind with the rest of the items in storage.

Saipan's average temperature was eighty-four degrees, and the ocean water was eighty-two. We got used to the warmth and felt chilled on stormy days when the thermometer dipped into the upper seventies. My sisters and I spent our mornings in homeschool, our mother strict about start hours and homework, and we spent our afternoons snorkeling in the lagoon.

My new best friend, Tammy Moen, lived across the street. We were both wild for crafts, any kind (I remember in particular a bloody incident that included streamers and a pair of sharp scissors), but I couldn't stop thinking about knitting. I missed the *snick-snick* of the needles slipping against each other and the feeling of yarn dragging across my little finger. I even missed the eternal dent in my first finger that came from shoving too-tight stitches off the end of the left needle. I was homesick for knitting. When I realized my mistake in leaving my yarn three thousand miles behind, I plunged myself into other crafts, trying to fill the void. I took classes at the local recreation department in palm-frond basket weaving and traditional Chamorro beading, but the delicate work wasn't enough to satisfy me. Joeten, the local supermarket, carried latch hook rug kits featuring hideous leopards and clowns. The stabbing motion of driving the hook through the mesh wasn't anything like knitting, and only frustrated me.

Then I learned that Grandma Moen, who lived in the one air-conditioned room of Tammy's concrete house, was holding. Along with cases of cigarettes, a gross of playing cards, and hundreds of Harlequin romances, she'd brought yarn to the island when they'd left the States a year before. She didn't have much, but she was generous with what she did have, letting me "borrow" skeins from her if I had a good reason.

And boy, did I have a reason: knitted gloves. I wanted them so badly I could almost feel them when I wiggled my fingers. Perhaps they weren't at all practical for a tropical island. But in the island's library, which only opened the third Saturday afternoon of every month, I'd found one thin pattern pamphlet. I had a choice between making gloves or a sweater, and I knew I couldn't ask to borrow enough yarn to make a cardigan.

Grandma Moen, who had lived in Minnesota and knew from cold, asked me what I'd do with gloves in eighty-four-degree heat. She stared at me piercingly, trying to see if I was worthy. Tammy was busy making a doll out of old pantyhose and wasn't paying attention.

"Someday I'll live someplace cold," I said. I didn't know if it was the right answer, but I dreamed about being grown up, living in New York, walking through Central Park in the snow on my way to a fabulous party.

"Would you like that?" she asked.

I loved Saipan's wet warmth, loved the way it felt on my face, and how the webs between my fingers never quite dried out. I loved the brilliant green of everything. I loved the almost-constant warm rain that fell in the wet season. I even liked the drama of the typhoons that swept the island with regularity, the way Dad would put up the storm boards and we'd test the batteries in the radio. The truth was, I never wanted to leave.

"Yes," I said. "I want to live in the snow someday." This, too, was true.

It was the right answer. She handed over the yarn.

Something about the fiddliness of shaping the fingers after knitting the wide tube of the hand was inherently pleasing to me, and I caught on quickly to the technique. I made the first green glove within two days, and the second one went even faster. I put them on and chased my little sister with them, telling her that I had monster hands. Six-year-old Bethany squealed in delight and climbed the trunk of the flame tree to escape my grasp. I turned around and strutted toward the boonies, the jungle edge of our yard, imagining a handsome man helping me up by my gloved hand into his carriage. I couldn't decide which was better, pretending to be a monster or dreaming about face-less men. Confused, and with sweaty, wool-covered palms, I chose both.

Shortly after I'd ripped out the gloves and started them over again, just to have something to knit, I got my first period. It was nothing like the books said it would be—it was messy, the cramps were painful, and God knows I'd have used tampons if I could have figured them out. But reading the applicator instructions by the light of a bath-room candle in the middle of one of the island's frequent blackouts didn't work for me, and I couldn't ask anyone—Tammy hadn't gotten her period yet, and I was too embar-rassed to ask my buttoned-up mother. It felt like I was misunderstanding something really important, and I felt ashamed and very young.

But I knew what I was doing when I was knitting. The yarn, a thin acrylic sock-weight, resisted pilling as if it were made of iron. I knitted and reknitted those gloves until the morning Mom called them my security blanket. Her words horrified me. I didn't need a childlike blankie for comfort—I was a woman now. I hid the knitting in a cardboard box under my bed. Just before I pushed it away to rest in darkness, I added the stuffed cat I'd shipped from home. I loved cuddling it at night, but grown-ups didn't cuddle stuffed animals. So I wouldn't either.

Time moved on. Mom and Dad marked our heights against the wall next to the louvered windows in the living room. We celebrated Christmas with a pathetic branch from the ironwood tree—Dad drilled holes in it and stuffed more branches in them, gluing them in place. It was the ugliest tree I'd ever seen, and it made me cry. I suffered through my first crush: Mario at the post office had kind eyes, only nine fingers, and never once noticed me.

I turned thirteen, and Dad decided twelve-year-old Christy and I were ready to learn how to drive. The quarried coral used in Saipan's roads made them light pink and slick as sin in the rain. Dad would take us to an unused strip of WWII airfield and have us speed up in the old Suzuki. At some point he'd scream, "Panic stop!" The goal was to stop as quickly as possible without losing control of the vehicle. Looking back, I can't believe a) we never flipped the car, and b) that Dad thought this was a good idea. I thought it was a *fantastic* idea, and after six months of practice, I was allowed to drive places by myself if I promised to be very careful. That clinched it. I was a grown-up. Driving a car proved it.

Early one September morning when Dad was off-island on business, we were woken by a phone call telling us to board up for the typhoon screaming across the Pacific in our direction. The western sea-facing windows of our house had no glass, only screens, so with help from neighbors, we covered them with plywood secured with heavy-duty six-inch nails. Then we took cover, hoping that the concrete walls and ceiling of our government house would hold strong. I thought it was exciting. I was the oldest daughter, and since Dad was gone, I was Mom's right hand. I told my sisters that everything would be all right. The brave words felt good in my mouth.

Super typhoons—those with sustained wind-speeds more than one hundred fifty miles per hour—don't occur often, but when they do, they devastate everything that gets in their way. Our tiny island lay directly in Super Typhoon Kim's path, and she tore into the island with terrifying ferocity. The eight-foot pieces of plywood shredded away from the house in splinters. As the rain began to fly horizontally through the house, and as the roof started to make ominous noises, my mother decided to evacuate us to the neighbor's house. It was a short run of perhaps twenty-five yards, and Mom gave us strict instructions to drop to the ground if the wind tried to pick us up. She gave charge of Bethany to me, and my chest puffed with pride before it sank in fear again at the roar of the storm.

The wind was so forceful inside the house that Mom could barely wrestle open the leeward door to shove us out. I tucked Bethany under my arm and ran. Later, even though the wind had ripped off one of her tightly tied tennis shoes, she said she never felt it. Mom, despite her warnings to drop to the ground, was picked up and blown into a palm tree, breaking a rib. Our neighbor crawled outside to drag her in, and we all huddled in the safest room until the eye passed over, the quiet terrifying in its suddenness. Then the wind returned, hitting us from the opposite direction. We learned later that the storm broke the island's wind-speed meter at 212 miles per hour.

When it was over, I walked behind my mother as we waded through our house, still knee-deep in water. I couldn't admit it to anyone, but I only wanted one thing: the box under my bed. I wanted that yarn and, just as badly, I wanted that old plush cat. I wanted to knit, dreaming of when I'd wear my gloves in Central Park, and at the same time I wanted to curl up with the cat and close my eyes, staying safe and warm and dry under my mother's watchful eye. I went first to my bed and pulled out the box, thrilled that the contents were only wet, that they hadn't floated away.

We didn't have running water for a week. Terrified of spiders and snakes and centipedes, I hated nothing more than having to go into the boonies to dig a hole to use as a latrine, so I tried to eat and drink as little as possible. It was a childish reaction, and I was ashamed of myself, but I couldn't help it. I was scared to be alone, half naked, in the jungle.

I followed my mother's lead, carrying clothes and food out into the now-beaming sun to lay them on the lawn to dry. Book by book, we spread their pages on the grass, trying to save beloved classics. It took days to set everything out, and I felt brave swallowing my tears like my mother did.

We still had a week before my father would return from

the States. I did what my mother asked me to, watching over Bethany and Christy when they wanted to play, and I helped clean and dry the house and our possessions as much we could. In daylight hours, I was strong. I think I was helpful. At night, without my father there to push back the black night, I was scared. Leaving the circle of candles in the living room and walking down the hall by myself, carrying one flickering candle to my bedroom, terrified me. Never scared of the dark before, I couldn't walk in front of darkened mirrors while carrying my candle without being convinced something would rise in the black glass, something that would kill me. The bathroom at night, already the site where I dealt with the blood that I hated, with its scary mirror, horrible centipedes, and occasional tiny scorpion, became the most frightening place in the house. I didn't feel grown up. I felt younger than six-year-old Bethany. *She* wasn't afraid to go to the bathroom by herself. I longed for the feeling of yarn in my hands, but the gloves were still outside, drying with everything else. I wanted to remake them. I wanted a do-over. I wasn't getting growing up right yet, and I wanted to give it another try.

One by one, things dried on the grass outside. We stacked our dry but warped books and laid bricks on top to weigh them down and help flatten them back into shape. When my stuff was finally dry, I hugged the plush cat and put it back in its box. I picked up the gloves, thinking about how much time I'd put into them, again and again. I pictured myself ten years hence—at twenty-three, I would probably be a famous writer and have fabulous friends and many lovers, all of whom would kiss me as passionately as the heroes kissed the heroines in Grandma Moen's romance novels. I might still knit, I decided, but by then I'd probably be knitting grown-up things: sweaters for boyfriends, fancy scarves for my friends.

Suddenly, gloves felt childish to me, like the cat did. I realized that I didn't need them anymore. I ripped the yarn back, rolling my former gloves into a neat ball. Every stitch I tugged out of the gloves was a wish. Every round I ripped represented another step I thought I was taking toward womanhood.

And then, without asking myself why, I grabbed the stuffed cat out of its box and put it back on my bed. It wasn't like it would *hurt* to keep it close at night.

Ten Years Later

Tammy and I reconnected a couple of years ago, and we recently spent time thinking about all the things her grandmother made. And I got to thank Tammy for providing me with a spare grandmother who taught me to love romance and yarn even more than I already did. She helped make me into who I am today: a (very mildly and only in certain circles) famous writer who has had many fabulous lovers and friends. The dream really did come true.

But I'm still scared of mirrors in dark rooms.

WRAP AND TURN

*I*n the late nineties, a time of wild excess and growth for the Bay Area, I secured my first solo apartment. It was a bad time to look for affordable housing —the dot-com boom lasted from 1995 to 2000, and I was searching in 1997, during the roundest, most expensive time of the financial bubble. Most tiny studio apartments were renting at more than a thousand dollars a month, and I could afford less than half that. I'd already speculated with my own credit getting my undergraduate degree, and I'd blown that endeavor quite spectacularly, so I was focused on living somewhere cheap in order to pay down some of my staggering debt. When I found my two-hundred-square-foot hovel in East Oakland for three hundred dollars a month, even with all its problems, I thought it was perfect.

I was finally living alone! I bought my very own dish drainer. I looked forward to knowing that I'd be the only person to eat the ice cream in the freezer. And I'd be by myself, writing. I was in grad school with the aim of learning how to use words to make beautiful things—sentences—that could be strung together to make something useful—books—for other people. I was pretty sure a degree wasn't going to make me lots of money, but I wanted to invent myself as a writer, the only thing I'd ever dreamed of becoming. I'd figure out how to make a living with the degree later, after I had it.

My new apartment hung under a garage on the steep slope of an Oakland hillside. The kitchen was only big enough to hold a three-quarter-size stove and a mini fridge, and the space I liked to call the sitting room was no more than four feet long by three feet wide. I could hold out my arms and touch both side walls. The ceiling was so low I could press my hands flat above me without rising up on tiptoe.

But it had a separate bedroom, and even though it wouldn't hold more than my desk and a twin bed, the mere fact that it wasn't a studio felt like the height of luxury. The bedroom jutted out from the sitting area, standing on stilts twelve feet above the ivy-covered slope below. Surrounded by trees on three sides, sitting at my computer, staring into tangles of greenery, I could convince myself that I wasn't a student living in an urban metropolis but a writer honing her craft alone in the forest.

While my friends joined start-ups and learned about wine, I planted my first garden with artichokes, tomatoes, basil, and nasturtiums. I adored sitting on my porch, smelling the jasmine I'd cultivated, admiring the way the foxgloves waved in the breeze.

My rental rate, however, reflected the care put into the property upkeep by my real-estate-speculator landlord.

During the course of my stay, the apartment suffered creeping mold, a tarantula invasion (yes, real tarantulas covered in red hair), an electrical fire, and many, many blocked sewer lines due to tree roots tangled in the pipes. While flushing, I'd frequently hear a gurgle just before the toilet started gushing waste into the bathroom.

But I handled all that myself when my landlord wouldn't return my calls. I could kill huge spiders, even furry ones. The fire was a small one, quickly extinguished, and the toilet . . . well, I had Roto-Rooter on speed dial.

What almost did me in, however, was the cold.

Normally I don't get cold. I'm usually the last person to put on a sweater and the first one to strip it off. But during the time I lived in my Oakland tree house, I couldn't warm up. Even in summer when it was ninety degrees outside, the rooms sucked the coldness out of the hill they were built into, and the damp crept into my bones in a way I'd never felt before. Winter, with its constant fog and rain, was harrowing. I never managed to fix all the holes surrounding the door and windows, and the curtains flapped as chilling winds outside swept in. Of course, I wasn't living in Alaska. I wasn't even near the Sierras. We didn't have snow. I wasn't ever in danger of freezing to death, but that didn't stop me from thinking that I might.

I tried just about everything to keep warm: fleece, an electric blanket, hot showers. I had a space heater that wheezed while emitting the smallest amount of heat imaginable, and some days I resorted to baking just so my miniature oven would heat up the small space. I learned how to make bread that first winter in an effort to stay warm. But nothing worked as well as wearing good old simple layers. And the best, warmest layers were made of wool.

Shivering at my desk, I wore two sweaters, two layers of sweatpants, and three layers of wool socks. As a final layer, I wrapped my terry cloth robe around myself and watched my breath between writing sentences. Realizing I didn't actually *own* enough woolen items, I sat on my wee green couch, only big enough for me and my cat, Digit, and knitted out of desperation. But with neither extra cash nor room for storage, it had been a while since I had stockpiled yarn, and after I'd made two hats (which I wore at the same time, pulling one over the other), I ran out of yarn.

Back then, my budget didn't even have room for cheese that didn't come in a yellow block. When I wasn't sitting at the tree house's window attempting to write the Coldest Great American Novel, I was slinging hash at the Oakland Grill, a popular breakfast joint downtown in the produce district. My customers were well-dressed young people my age who were buying lofts in Jack London Square and talking about mind share and venture capital. They didn't notice me except when they needed more mimosas brought to their booths. It took a long time to pool the dollar tips into what I needed to pay bills, and there wasn't much left over for frivolous purchases. (I'll admit there was, usually, enough for a drink or two after work down at Merchant's, the blue-collar dive bar in the produce district that the tech industry kids were too scared to walk into.)

But more than alcohol or other frivolous purchases, I needed wool. And I needed it cheap.

Inspiration came while I was shopping with a friend in a department store. It wasn't my kind of place—it sold purses worth more than my first two cars put together. Janice, a successful tech writer for a microchip company in Silicon Valley, was in the fitting room, and I was wandering around, idly touching racks full of things I couldn't afford, when my fingers hit it: a cashmere sweater on the sale rack, thick and warm. Even on sale, it was still out of my price range, but I yanked at its seams, peering at its construction.

When she came out of the dressing room, I looked at her in amazement. "I could take this apart."

"Why?" She looked horrified as she examined the label. "It's cashmere."

"That's the point. It's an ugly fit, and even on sale it's fifty bucks, so I'm not buying it. But if I did, I could take it apart and make something else. Look here—it's been machine knitted in pieces. That means it would unravel into cashmere yarn!"

Janice looked around to see if anyone had heard us. "I'll get it for you, but only if you don't take it apart. You can't buy a sweater in order to make a different sweater."

"That's *exactly* what I want to do." I didn't let her buy it for me, though. I had a better idea. I could find *cheaper* sweaters. I wasn't my frugal parents' daughter for nothing. "I'm going to Goodwill. Wanna come?"

"No," she said, getting out her Amex Black Card. "Thanks."

I went on my own. And I was right. The sweaters at the thrift store were plentiful and cheap. Most of them were acrylic—this was California, after all, not Alaska. But in among the tacky holiday sweaters decorated with snowmen and wreaths were genuine woolen prizes that made my eyes light up brighter than a kid finding a bike under the Christmas tree. I pushed aside a Santa sweater and found an oversized fisherman's sweater made of cream-colored wool with a small brown stain at the neck. I wouldn't need all the yarn anyway. I could just throw out that blemished bit when I unraveled to it. It worked. I re-knit that garment into a smaller gansey that fit me perfectly. An Old Navy men's sweater that was hideous in its drop-shoulder construction yielded enough yarn to make a fitted cardigan and a matching hat. My thrift store finds were my own personal Christmas morning, come early.

While the new sweaters helped, I was still cold. I was knitting my hands off, but I was so bundled up that I could barely bend my arms to hold the needles, the ineffective space heater clicking and sighing at my feet. And I could still see my breath. I'd move from the couch, where my knitting was, to my desk, where I'd peck out more sentences while jiggling my legs in an effort to generate heat. It helped when Digit sat on my lap, but sometimes he shivered too. To combat the frigid air, I needed something more, something bigger.

At this point, I had a collection of thrift store sweaters and, one by one, I frogged them (so called for the sound it makes when you rip it, *rippit*), snipping seams and winding the crimped yarn into unequal balls. I cast three hundred stitches onto a forty-four-inch size seven needle, and I knitted back and forth, making a simple garter stitch blan-ket, changing colors every four rows. The narrow strips of color gradually layered on top of each other in stripes that I found soothing.

And the best side effect of knitting a blanket? No matter who you're planning on warming with it in the end, as soon as it's more than about twenty inches long, it keeps you warm while you knit. I grew to love the weight of it on my lap, and Digit ducked under it, sleeping in the pocket of warmth created between my thigh and the couch. I kept it with me as I shuffled between couch and desk, knitting stitches when I was stumped for words, and when it got long enough to be called done, I put it on the bed—and started another one. During those cold years, I felt like I was the only one in the world doing what I was doing. Surely someone else in the Bay Area was writing, knitting, cooking, and gardening, but I didn't know her.

At school, I was surrounded by people who could afford to be in an expensive grad program and *just* focus on their degree. Sure, some of them tutored on the side, but I was the only student I knew who had to work full time. I served coffee and biscuits to dot-commers who were so casual with money that they'd sometimes leave fifty-dollar tips on a twenty-five-dollar meal. (Yay! My utilities were paid for a month!) I drove a crappy Ford Festiva with a broken tape deck and joked that if I had two, I'd have roller skates. I'm not ashamed to admit that I really had no idea how speculation worked in the dot-com industry that surrounded me. I just knew not to drive south on Interstate 880 in the mornings, or I'd sit in bumper-to-bumper traffic, surrounded by new BMWs and Saabs heading to Silicon Valley. In my chilly tree house, I felt isolated—was I screwing my life up? Doing it all wrong?

I had a sinking feeling the book I was writing wouldn't turn out to be, actually, the Great American Novel. But I just kept writing, hoping I'd figure it out somehow. The blankets I knitted weren't actually that attractive, but I kept knitting because they were warm. I tried to believe in my broke, indebted, tree house–living self, even while I sat on the porch next to my artichoke plant watching the Roto-Rooter guy try to figure out the drains again.

I graduated just before the dot-com crash. I left my academic ivory tower and got a real job, with benefits. I could afford to move into an apartment with a real heater. I had too many blankets even for me, and a few of them went back to the same thrift store where they'd lived in a former incarnation. I bought a used car that had power windows and a CD player. As I became a little more upwardly mobile, others came down in the crash, and then we all hung out in the same bars, the same cheap breakfast places, just like we all splurged on a nice meal once in a while. More of my friends starting growing vegetables and making their own pasta from scratch.

I was still knitting, of course. While socks grew from my needles, for the first time people stopped laughing at my grandma-hobby and started asking, "Hey, is that hard?"

"It can be frustrating to learn the basic moves, but once you have them, it's easy."

"Could you show me?"

I'd smile, warmth creeping through me like I had a cat-weighted blanket on my chest, like the sun was shining on my shoulders, like I'd slid into a warm bubble bath. "I'd love to."

DOUBLE CROCHET

*J*ohn and I met in Amsterdam, two American twenty-somethings high on the thrill of back-packing across Europe (and maybe a little something else). We kissed in Dam Square under a full moon, and went even further on the hostel's balcony, trains racing past us just yards away. Before he put me on the train to go to my next city, he told me he'd seen a wedding gown in a window and thought it would suit me.

Once we were back in the States, it was clear this was more than a travel fling. Even though he lived and worked in Montana, and I lived in California while finishing my undergraduate degree, we managed to see each other at least once a month for a few days—it would keep us on track, John felt.

From the beginning, John knew we were meant to be. But he wouldn't propose until the moment was right, he said, until we'd reached the correct moments in our sepa-rate lives. I thrilled to the words, but for some reason never imagined an actual wedding. The months ticked by, and my frequent flier miles added up. Three years of short flights made me tired of packing my suitcase, but I loved John. I wanted to be with him as often as I could, yet, at the same time, I loved being at home.

I started to feel like I had two separate lives. At home in the Bay Area, I felt independent and wild. I smoked. I drank with strangers in bars and flirted inappropriately. But when I went to visit John, I could feel myself changing, sometimes while still on the airplane. He was the first to admit he was judgmental, to the point where he usually thought models could stand to lose some weight. He was critical of my body, of both its size and shape. Though I knew he loved me, the closer I got to him, the less pretty I felt. My face looked fatter in my compact mirror. Stepping off the plane and hauling my size twelve self up into his Jeep, I felt less competent. Not as smart. I craved cigarettes with every fiber of my being, but he hated smoking, so when I visited him, I pretended I'd given it up.

Little did John know that when he left for work, I'd listen for the creak of the garage door and watch the Jeep leave while peeking through a crack in the Venetian blinds. Then I'd go out to his porch and light up while looking at the distant Rockies. I stood upwind, moving as the wind changed, dancing with my illicit smoke. When I was done, I tamped it out on tinfoil I brought onto the porch with me, then wrapped the butt up tightly so I could toss it in a neighbor's trash can. Inside, I washed my hands and face and brushed my teeth so hard my gums bled. John said that he had a sensitive nose, that he could always detect cigarette smoke on people. He never once smelled the lie on me.

I was doing a lot of undetectable lying, in fact. And a lot of traveling. What I wasn't doing was knitting. I'd become so confused about who I was that I'd forgotten some of my favorite things about myself. I never made John a sweater, citing the boyfriend curse (the notion that if one makes a sweater for a boyfriend, the relationship is doomed), but that was a lie too: the truth was I didn't *want* to knit for him. I didn't want to knit for anyone. I'd lost the appetite for yarn entirely. The only creative thing I could do was write, and that itself felt like a stretch. I'd even lost the ability to make entries in my journal, because whatever I wrote felt false, angry, untrue, and unnatural.

In class, I studied again one of my favorite stories, Charlotte Perkins Gilman's "The Yellow Wallpaper," written almost exactly one hundred years before, and I identified as I never had before with the narrator, unreliable as she was, dealing with her John. Gilman's words spoke to me as if she'd written the story for me: *John is practical in the extreme.* Oh, yeah. An extreme libertarian, my John kept in his house a stockpile of everything he might need in case the government failed. *I suppose John never was nervous in his life.* My John never dithered. He was always sure of himself. *It does exhaust me a good deal—having to be so sly about it, or else meet with heavy opposition.* I was getting confused by my lies, almost tripped up so often that I stopped calling him as frequently, not trusting myself to get my stories right. *I get unreasonably angry with John sometimes. I'm sure I never used to be so sensitive.*

I could feel his unspoken criticism when he looked at me, and I'd repeatedly change my clothes until his face relaxed and I knew I looked as skinny as possible. I did things in bed I didn't want to do so I wouldn't lose him. Every moment we were together, I wondered if I could keep from flying apart. Lost, and feeling as trapped behind bars as Gilman's protagonist had been, I had become an unreliable narrator too. I restricted my writing to fiction, spinning webs of lies—it was the only thing I could think of to do.

I cry at nothing, and cry most of the time.

I entered a short story in my college's creative writing contest. To my astonishment, "The Yellow Afghan," named in homage to Gilman, won third place. About a woman lost while following her dreams who wraps herself up in an afghan to cry, it wasn't a great story, but winning the small accolade confirmed my desire to pursue writing. I'd applied to Mills College's MFA program, and I was considering moving to Oakland in the fall.

John loved that I wanted my master's degree. Honestly, he loved it more than I did. He had his master's from Yale and believed in higher education for anyone he spent time talking to. In one late-night phone conversation, my feet propped up on the wall, my head hanging off my bed, I asked, "Would you still want to be with me if I just finished school now, with my bachelor's degree?"

He said, "Well . . ."

I sat up, my head spinning from coming up too fast. "You wouldn't? Really?"

He coughed and then said, "I just always thought I'd end up with someone who had as much education as I did."

I cried silently into the phone, blaming hiccups for the funny sound. The next day, I mailed in my acceptance letter to Mills. I wanted, *needed*, his approval, while at the same time I was sickened by how small that neediness made me feel.

Besides, it is such an undertaking to go so far. I don't feel as if it was worthwhile to turn my hand over for anything, and I'm getting dreadfully fretful and querulous.

Even after I started graduate work, I wasn't sure what the hell I was going to do with an advanced degree in writing. I only knew one thing: nothing I did felt authentic. I was failing at my relationship, even if I was the only one who knew it. I was behind in my bills. I fought bronchitis constantly, a side effect of living in a moldy apartment with a pack-a-day habit. And whenever I disembarked in Montana to see John, I knew I was lying to him and, worse, to myself, about practically everything. I pretended to be cheerful. I acted like I was happy. I kissed him as if I felt it and made love even though I didn't want to.

John must have picked up on my emotions—he started to worry about my fidelity, and though I was a good liar, he had valid reason to be worried. I was casting about at home, too, trying to find myself in whatever—and whoever —came near me. I was lost in the wallpaper of my own making.

John does not know how much I really suffer. He knows there is no reason to suffer, and that satisfies him.

I went to see my John at Christmas. I can't remember now what I gave him, but it was probably something prosaic: a nice pen, maybe, or a jacket. When I unwrapped my gift from him, I didn't understand it at first. It was an afghan. A bright yellow crocheted afghan. *Oh,* I thought, *like my first published story. How sweet.*

"I love it," I said. "Where did you get it?"

He grinned that full-body smile I'd fallen in love with, and my heart thumped with reckless hope. "I made it. I bought a book and taught myself, and I've spent the last two months making it for you. I worked on it every night when I got home and for hours every weekend. Do you like it?"

Did I like it? It was the best, sweetest, most considerate gift I'd ever received, bar none. And I didn't deserve it. *I* was the crafter, and I'd never even made him so much as a scarf. I pulled John's afghan around myself, and finally, swathed in yarn for the first time in a long time, I felt something like strength begin to fill me. I started to remember, dimly, who I was. Who I'd been.

There is one marked peculiarity about this paper, a thing nobody seems to notice but myself, and that is that it changes as the light changes.

Back home in California, I bought yarn for the first time in a long time. Casting on for a cardigan for myself felt like stepping out of a dark room into the light. As my fingers caught the rhythm of the needles, I caught the rhythm of my thoughts, and I was able to write, not just fiction, but in my journal again too. I wrote, "I'm not sure what to do about John, but something's wrong." It was true, and when it was on the page, I had to look at it. "I can't do this to myself much longer."

As the sweater grew on my lap, something strange happened. When I tried to lie, I stuttered and stammered and turned bright red. Since I'd been with John, I'd been able to lie so cavalierly, without thought of consequence. Now, every stitch mattered and each word meant something.

Ending things with John was horrible. I broke his heart, breaking mine in the process as well—I still loved him, even though I didn't want to. Perched on an antique chair covered with roses in a dreadful bed-and-breakfast, I clutched my knitting needles and kept telling him the truth. John had never liked tattoos—I pulled up my sleeve and showed him I'd gotten my first one. It was a woman's symbol made of a ball of yarn and a pen, and the permanent ink made me feel free. I told him I wasn't even sure I was completely straight. I told him I'd slept with someone else. He didn't have to know how many someones there had been in my quest to see my worth reflected in someone else's eyes.

The front pattern does move—and no wonder! The woman behind shakes it!

The ever-truthful John sat there, stunned. I wasn't proud of my past actions, but I was proud as hell that I'd changed direction, that I was taking back the reins of my life, and, by God, I would make myself into a better person. None of it was his fault—he hadn't asked me to be anyone but myself. But I thought he had—every time he'd criticized a star on the screen for being too heavy, I'd measured myself to her and found myself heavier, uglier. Every time he'd praised the genius of a writer, I wondered if I could write those lines and knew that no, I couldn't. So I'd pretended for years, trying to be better, smarter, thinner, prettier, more perfect than the actual real person I should have been—the only person I was good at being: me. I'd disguised who I was for years, and when I found the woman behind the wallpaper was actually myself, I felt only relief.

He says no one but myself can help me out of it, that I must use my will and self-control.

After I asked John to leave for the last time, I curled up on my tiny twin bed, the yellow blanket wrapped tight around me. The yarn cut into my fingers, but the pain was mine, and I didn't mind it. I imagined sweaters I'd make myself, journals I'd fill with authentic thoughts, lovers I'd take without lying. It would be easy to say the afghan he gave me saved me by reminding me who I was, where I came from, but it didn't. It did, however, cushion my fall.

*T*en Years Later
I know you'll understand this: I kept that blanket for way too long because someone had *made* it for me. Not once did I ever drape it over my legs or wrap it around my shoulders—it stayed in its permanent spot on the shelf below all the other blankets that actually got used.

Then, one day, I really listened to the slight groan my soul gave whenever my eye fell on it.

I gave the afghan to Goodwill.

BACKSTITCH

hile cruising the yarn world on my laptop some years ago, the word *Ashburton* jumped out at me as if it were blinking neon. Ashburton, a tiny town in the South Island of New Zealand, is the home of the famed Ashford spinning wheel, as well as my mother's childhood home. I immediately ordered wool to make her a sweater. It wouldn't be fancy. Made of rugged, stiff wool, it would be brown with blue and green stripes. It would be boxy, knitted in garter stitch—nothing delicate or intricate in its design—and would match the sturdy woman I was making it for. I loved my mother, of course. She was my little mama. But I didn't know her very well, and I decided that by knitting her a sweater out of New Zealand wool, I might get a better understanding of where she came from.

Mom didn't share memories freely, but I tried to coax as many stories about her life on her father's sheep farm as I could. I knew, for example, that she loved dogs but was never allowed to have one as a pet—to her father, dogs were meant to work, not meant to be indoors. I was pretty sure she'd told me once that it had been bitter cold when she'd been away at boarding school in Timaru as a child, but later I couldn't remember if her suffering from chilblains was a true detail gleaned from her or one I'd imported into my memory from reading *Jane Eyre*.

As a child, I loved picturing my mother in such a completely different environment—she had known lambing and shearing and all things woolly. She'd been allowed to help when she could, but since her father died while she was still young, that wasn't often. My grandfather was a mystery to me—I could barely imagine him. All I could picture was the man I called Grandpa George, my mother's stepfather. To me, George was my grandfather and her only father, and to think that she'd had a different one before him boggled my brain.

"What was your father like?" I asked my mother when I was about sixteen. She was at the sink, rinsing dishes, and I was at the kitchen table, ostensibly working on math homework. I longed for anything to take my mind off the agony of my textbook. I didn't really expect an answer. Mom was deft at sidestepping questions.

But this time she paused, placing the plate in the dish drainer deliberately before answering me. "His left hand was hard like a farmer's, but his right hand was soft. Like a woman's."

"Why?"

"Every night as the sheep came in, he'd count them to make sure they were all there. As they came past the stile with the dogs driving them, he'd touch the back of each one, so his right hand was always coated in lanolin." Mom looked out the kitchen window into the night, as if seeing something that I couldn't see, something that I wanted to understand.

"What was that like, living on the sheep farm?"

She looked back down at the sink. I'd pushed too far. "How's the math going?" she asked.

Still, it was more than I usually got. It never struck me how little I knew of my mother until a mutual friend commented on their relationship. Ruth was the manager of the bookstore where Mom and I both worked.

"You know, I think your mom's one of my best friends," she said. "Jan knows everything about me. And I don't know one damn thing about her."

I was vaguely surprised and didn't understand why she'd said it. Then, the more I thought about it, the more I realized that I didn't know my mother either. I had a little knowledge of her upbringing and her travels before she met my father, but when it came to stories, the kind everyone tells, the once-upon-a-time stories, I didn't know any. She didn't tell them.

So when I found yarn from Ashford made from Corriedale sheep, the very breed her father had raised along with South Downs, I was elated. I imagined that perhaps the sheep that bore the wool I bought had grazed the same land her father had tended. The sheep could very literally be the progeny of the ones she'd known as a child. Finally, I'd found a gift I could give her that had real meaning.

Christmas came. Mom opened her package. She pulled the sweater out and said, "Oh, how lovely."

"It's from Ashburton," I cried.

"Really?"

"From Corriedales. Like your dad raised!" I waited for her to yelp with joy, to cover me in kisses, to weep from emotion.

But instead, she smiled and said, "Thank you so much. I love it." And that was that.

She wore the sweater sometimes. I have a picture of her with me and my sister standing on her back porch in the sunshine—all three of us are wearing sweaters I knitted, she in the brown New Zealand wool one. My mother was the kind of person who wore her clothes for decades. If a piece of clothing had any life in it at all, she kept putting it on her body until the holes were irreparable, and then the clothing was cut into strips and used as rags.

After she died too young at sixty-eight, my sisters and I proved to be good at divvying up her possessions. I'd heard stories of families ripped apart when heirs fought over estates, but we didn't. We went through her few pieces of jewelry calmly in a fair distribution. We were equitable when claiming favorite dish towels.

If necessary, however, I was prepared to lock my sisters in a room and run out the front door with the thing I wanted clutched to my chest: the knitting. I wanted the green vest I'd given to her when it turned out to look ridiculous on me, and I got it. I wanted the hand-spun lace scarf I'd designed for her, and my sisters let me have it. And I kept waiting, as we went through her things, to find the Ashburton sweater.

We didn't find it. It wasn't anywhere in the house, not in the closets or the cedar chests. Her old acrylic sweaters were all there, including the cream one with the coffee stain in the middle of the chest, and the gray striped one with the holes in the sleeves that had never fit her well. But the one I made her was gone.

She wouldn't have given it to anyone. She wouldn't have put it in a bag for Goodwill. The only logical answer left was that she had lost it. Jan Herron, however, did not lose things. If not in the ignition, her keys were in her purse in the same side pocket. Her reading glasses rested in their case next to the bed. She'd rarely misplaced as much as a comma.

So if she lost the sweater, which I believe is what happened, the corollary was that she kept the loss from me. An action occurred that she then covered up. By not mentioning it to me, it was as if it didn't happen.

What did that say about her? So much of her previous life, her life in New Zealand, in Germany, in Western Samoa, was unspoken, and therefore, unknown. Private. It's not as if I think there were dark secrets she was hiding. I never got the sense that she was abused as a child or that she was a drug-addled teenager. But everything she left unsaid remains a question in my mind. What else didn't I know?

When I was eighteen, my mother gave me a gold and platinum diamond ring that had been her Great-Aunt Lucy's. I asked for her story, but Mom didn't tell me. I lost the ring when I was twenty. Deeply upset, I searched everywhere for it, but I didn't tell my mother for a year. When I finally confessed that it was gone, she went to her room and dug around in her jewelry box, coming up with my ring.

"I found this while vacuuming," she said.

"When?" I sniffled, happy tears in my eyes, and slid the ring onto my finger.

"Oh, months and months ago."

"Why didn't you *tell* me?"

She shrugged. "If you didn't want to tell me you'd lost it, that was your business, not mine."

I had loved thinking of her during the winter, wrapped warmly in a sweater I'd made her, and it made me sad that she might have lost it and kept it from me on purpose. It makes me sadder to think of all the secrets she had wrapped up in her body, tales that I'll never hear told. I know, for example, that she loved a man in Germany named Gert—he'd written a letter to her in German on the front marbled endpaper of a German book of love songs. The first words were all I understood: *Mein Liebchen*, which I knew meant "my darling." She'd told me perhaps someday she'd translate the rest for me, but she never did. I played piano from the book after she died, and it made me cry knowing I'd never know Gert's story.

The last time we were together in New Zealand, she and I took a long walk. It was night in Coromandel, and there was no moon. We walked in almost complete darkness along the bay, a hill rising sharply to our right. If we peered into the ferny growth, glowworms lit up the greenery with a pale, eerie light. At the end of the road, we found a closed gas station and a payphone, and I learned Mom had an objective I hadn't known about. She pulled out a scrap of paper and used a calling card to call a man who had given her a guitar when she was in her early twenties. I think he was her first love. I walked up the road to give her privacy, and the wind started up. As I studied the glowworms and tried not to be frightened by the blackness of the night and the water, I heard her laugh float over the roaring wind. When she'd finished the call, she told me in a rare moment of confidence that he'd lost his wife many years ago to cancer. We turned to walk back and I tried to tease more from her.

"You should keep in touch with him," I said, hating the sadness in her voice. "Did you get his email address?"

"No," she said. "I'll never talk to him again." It was all she would say. We walked back together to the hostel, both of us chilled by the night wind.

My mother just didn't talk about loss. She didn't speak of the loss of Gert or of the boy who gave her the guitar. I never saw her cry when her mother died, and she didn't speak of missing friends long gone. After her favorite cat, Rowena, died, we barely heard her name mentioned again. She didn't talk about my lost ring, and she never confessed the loss of the sweater I gave her, the sweater that symbolized her lost country. But her stories were her business, no one else's, not even her children's. And as difficult as that was for someone like me, who loves to talk about loss, to accept, I have. I won't ever know the stories. But it doesn't stop me from wishing I did.

Ten Years Later
This update is a doozy. I thought about taking this essay out, actually, but I'm letting it stand because it still says what I meant to say: that I didn't know my mother even though I loved her with all my heart.

But I got this essay wrong.

Shortly after I had a hysterectomy at thirty-nine, my sisters went south to go through some boxes that had somehow been overlooked when we tried to go through Mom's things after she died. It turned out there were a lot of boxes.

Guess what they found?

The sweater I made her.

In the first edition of this book, I wrote about lost things, and wondered how a mother devoted to losing nothing could lose something I knew she cherished.

Yeah. She *didn't* lose it.

I'm rolling my eyes at myself. I should have known.

The sweater was just neatly packed away in the garage. She died in June; she'd probably packed it with her other winter woolens in April or so. Twice a year, she went through her closet and packed up the out-of-season wear to wait for the appropriate temperature to roll around again. How could I have not thought of that? She loved routines. File folders. Lists.

My sisters also brought some more of her writing to me. We shared that, Mom and I. Both of us wanted to be writers so badly and we both achieved that dream. In fact, before either of us was published, she took me to my first writing conference at Cuesta Community College in San Luis Obispo. We went to the same classes, and both of us took detailed notes that we saved. We ate lunch in the cafeteria and goggled at the published writers (she was more suave than I was, having met many of the local authors through her bookstore jobs).

And sitting with her papers, I found her most authentic voice, the one I'd been looking for for years. It was in a surprising place. She published dozens of articles and wrote a newspaper column for years. Every time I'd read a piece, I'd start with hope and then begin skimming, hoping for the meat. The feeling. The fear, the joy, the loss, the confusion, the happiness.

Instead, Mom wrote like a journalist. Everything was beautifully well-written and impeccably well-researched. When asked to present a speech on her most recent trip to New Zealand to the Arroyo Grande Ladies' Club, she prepared a talk on the history of the islands, not on what I hoped I'd find: how she felt about seeing her own mother's grave for the first time. When she wrote about going through Super-Typhoon Kim, she discussed how to dry books on a lawn after a 200+ mph typhoon, not how it *felt* to live through something that could have killed us all.

Then I opened her file folder from the creative writing class she took a few years before she died. And in the handwritten, incomplete essays, I found my little mama. She started an essay about the typhoon by saying she "was as frightened as I've ever been in my life." She remembered giggling with her friend Helen in the forties as her father drove them to the beach, a once-a-year delight. In an essay about her daughters' high school graduations, it's what she doesn't say that's telling. She starts to write how she was a bit more teary when her second daughter Christy crossed the podium—but then she stops and veers to a description of how girls in heels tottered on the grassy football field. She automatically self-censors something that might be wrong to share (but it's okay, Mom! Christy was valedictorian in a school of 2,000! We were all more teary that day).

It makes me think about my own writing. No one

would ever accuse me of not sharing my feelings. It's possible I share them too much. But in the same way she kept to herself, because it was what made her feel good, I run to the blog, or to my journal, to drop my feelings all over the place because it's what makes me feel whole.

Feelings like: I'd been blue, and I thought it was the hormones (or lack thereof). Running had been helping, and I was exercising every single day, and monitoring my moods as best I could. See how easy that was for me to tell you? Although my menopause was surgical and not natural, I didn't know how my mother's was, because I never asked her and she didn't volunteer things like that. (People with ovaries, call your mothers if you can. Ask.) I don't know if she got depressed, and I don't know if she had terrible hot flashes or not. Did she lose sleep? Did her migraines stop? Not knowing made me sad, which was exactly what I was trying to crawl out of, and *there I did it again* with the telling you about how I felt reading her writing.

But that's what we want, as people, right? We want to know how others feel because we're all basically sweetly selfish at the core, and we want to compare those feelings to our own to see if we're normal, to see if we're okay.

Then, in the back of that class's binder, I found a complete, typed essay for the class on how my middle name was almost Shea, after the dump-truck driver who helped my father make sure she was safely out of the Corvair they'd been trapped inside during a flood. My mother, full-term with me, couldn't climb out the window as my father had done. After Shea helped get her out, a helicopter (the dump truck's boss) followed them overhead as they walked home through the water to make sure they got there safely.

I loved that essay. And then I noticed its title, and I pretty much came undone. She might not have talked much about emotion, but when she did, she could fit it all into one word.

It was titled, simply, "Happiness."

CIRCULAR KNITTING

*I*n my twenties, I loved smoking. Really. I was *passionate* about cigarettes. I loved everything about them. I adored that first tang of sulfur when the match was blown out, the initial draw, the long middle, that last sour, greedily sucked, butt-end puff. I loved that smoking gave me an excuse to sit and do nothing. Seven minutes of silence is precious. Other times, smoking gave me something to hide behind. Like in all the best Bogie movies, the way a person holds her cigarette tells you something about her, and my smoking said *I'm not scared.* But of course, that wasn't true.

I'm not normally a very shy person, but in highly social settings, I get nerves so badly that I have to have something to grip, something to anchor me down. During my twenties, that something was smoking. At parties, I was the one who first got a glass of wine from the host and then immediately went to stand outside with the other socially awkward addicts. There was a bond among us, an agreement reached when we lit each other's cigarettes with the tips of our own. We understood each other. And the fact that we looked like cool kids smoking outside when we really were just nervous was a lie we'd keep to ourselves.

I had tried to quit many times before, but I had a pack-a-day habit, and I failed, again and again. I'd make the final resolution. *This* was the time it would work. No more! I'd crush out my last smoke, and feel victorious.

An hour later, I'd be in the car driving toward the gas station. *Don't do it don't do it don't do it.* The chant would stay in my head even as I opened my mouth and asked for the Marlborough Gold 100s, even as I handed my money to the cashier. *Don't do it don't*—I'd use the car's cigarette lighter and then I'd take a puff of failure and consider throwing out the rest of the pack, but it was four hard-earned dollars, how could I do that?

I know it sounds stupid, but quitting felt like losing a friend. No, worse. It felt like losing twenty of my best little filter-tipped friends, all standing at attention in my purse, always there for me, ready to get me out of sticky situations, to ease the stresses of everyday life. If I quit, what would I hide behind?

Just before I turned thirty, I was knitting at work, as I often did. I worked 911, and the lines were slow. My two coworkers and I were chatting—I was about to ask if I could go outside and have a smoke.

Lisa said, "What are you making again?"

I held up a yellow sleeve. "Sweater."

"God, you must save so much money making your own clothes."

Before I could even snort and start to correct this common misbelief, Nichole said, "Ha, like Rachael cares?

She doesn't have kids. She's got money to burn. Just look at all those cigarettes she buys."

Bristling, I twisted in my seat to glare at her. I did *not* have money to burn. Deep in debt, money worries kept me from sleeping at night. At that moment, 911 saved the day by ringing, and I talked to a woman about a loud party that was keeping *her* awake, instead of snapping at my coworker.

But Nichole was right, and I knew it. I was literally burning money by smoking, and hurting myself in the process. Lisa thought I could *save* money by knitting, but I could barely afford to buy yarn on top of my rent, utilities, and cigarette bills.

It hit me then.

What if I *bribed* myself to quit?

If I quit, I could buy as much yarn as I wanted. Everything. The finest merino, baby alpaca—even cashmere wouldn't be off-limits. I would knit *more*—for every second I ached to smoke, I'd knit and when I ran out of yarn, I'd simply buy more.

Would it work?

The Mayo Clinic in Minnesota says that keeping the hands busy by taking up knitting can help with quitting smoking, and med-school doctors note that knitting lowers your heart rate, your blood pressure, and your breaths per minute. Knitting *had* always been soothing to me and, maybe, just maybe, it would offer me the same shelter that smoking had. Even better, I would be doing something productive rather than destructive.

So I bought yarn like sheep were going bald, and I kept

the sock yarn in my purse in the same spot my cigarettes had been.

And to my surprise and delight, this time quitting smoking stuck.

Yarn was a different, healthier lifeline, and hey, I got to knit indoors! As a smoker I'd always been outside huddled in the cold and rain.

Every time I craved a cigarette, I pulled out my yarn. I made more socks that first year than I'd made in the previous ten years.

Sock knitting is almost entirely thoughtless knitting. I don't like fancy, lacy, patterned socks. My socks are just good old stockinette tubes with a heel and a ribbed cuff. I like the challenge of having to concentrate on sweaters and shawls, but I'm not looking for anything complicated when it comes to the socks I carry around in my purse. I just need them to be there for me, whether I'm stuck in line at the post office, or at a party chatting with people I barely know.

More than just helping me remain calm, smoking had always been a literal screen to hide behind when I felt something worse than feeling stressed: when I felt inadequate. If I tripped off a curb, I'd light up a cigarette and laugh it off. If I was unsure about the right answer to a question, I'd take a casual puff while considering my best options. I'd pretend that I was cool when, really, I was feeling woefully underprepared. I knew I wasn't cool. It was just another lie I told myself about smoking—in my heart of hearts I knew I was killing myself and looking like an asshole at the same time. But I hid behind the smoke regardless, ignoring that voice, until I quit and picked up the needles in desperation.

Now in my late thirties and still smoke-free, I was reminded of this recently, when I was signing books at the Oakland Fiber and Textile Festival. It was a gorgeous day in the Bay Area, the first really warm day of the summer. People frolicked in summer sundresses and shorts, slathering on the first layers of summer sunscreen. Children laughed and ran in the grass while knitters congregated under large umbrellas, admiring each other's work.

I sat at a small table with the occasional lanolin-scented breeze wafting by. I got to meet readers, see friends, and sign books, all the while knitting socks in green Miss Babs yarn with blue heels and toes.

But even though it was awesome, it was still scary to sit out in the open with my first published novel at my elbow, people riffling through it and choosing to either buy it or walk on. So instead of staring at people perusing my book and making them squirm, I knitted. They were able to look at the front cover, flip it over and read the back, look at the quotes, and think about the price, while I hid behind my yarn, available for answering questions, avoiding the hard sell.

What they didn't know was that every time I frowned and looked down, fiddling with something on the needle, I was faking it.

Unless I'm turning the heel, I don't have to look at my knitting when working socks, which makes them a great portable project for social activities. When you can carry on a whole, uninterrupted conversation while maintaining eye contact, no one minds if you knit. In fact, the non-knitters are kind of impressed.

But it doesn't feel impressive. To me, it feels necessary for survival, in exactly the way cigarettes used to.

So when two knitting sisters suddenly started arguing next to my table, one saying she'd heard of my book, the other saying, no, she hadn't, she was thinking of another book, I squinted at my yarn as if I'd dropped a stitch while the sisters bickered. They argued the relative merit of knitting fiction as a whole while I kept my head down and my eyes on my work. To them, I looked engrossed, while in reality, I was just doing the knit stitch, over and over, around and around. I could have easily done this if I'd been dropped down a pitch-black well. I was so grateful to have my sock—I was hiding in plain sight, just like I used to with cigarettes. Everyone ignores the girl who's smoking and leaning against the concrete wall; no one makes eye contact. I loved that knitting brought me back that anonymity. The sisters didn't notice me (or buy the book, for that matter).

I hadn't thought ahead, though. After an hour, I finished my sock. Worse, it was the second one, so I couldn't just cast on again with the same yarn. I thought of doing something I've done in the past, which is to knit on with no regard for what the actual length was meant to be, planning to rip out the excess when safely behind closed doors, but I knew I had three more hours to sit at my book table, and I couldn't bear the thought of later having to rip out five inches of useless sock.

And I couldn't even consider my only other option: not knitting. Oh, no. Impossible. To sit and talk to strangers about my writing? Without knitting? No way. I looked jealously at the skater kid who cruised past on the sidewalk, cigarette clamped between his lips. I had a sudden urge to knock him off the board and take it from him. It wasn't an urge I'd ever act on, but I *could* just bum one like I used to. Did people still offer a quarter in the hopes it would be turned down per the smoker's agreement that someday everyone needs a smoke? What did people offer now that cigarette prices had doubled?

I had a flutter or two of panic in my chest as my stomach somersaulted.

Then I looked around: I was surrounded by table after table of yarn vendors.

Duh.

The panic went away, and I felt the cool assuredness that comes right before a yarn purchase. It honestly felt the same way that first drag used to feel: a sweet relief flowing through the bones, the knowledge that it was going to be okay. I crossed to the nearest booth and grabbed the closest sock-weight yarn. I didn't care what color it was, or what its fiber composition was, I just cared that I could cast on. Immediately.

I lucked out. The yarn was gorgeous: Amy Klimt's hand-dyed merino/cashmere/Tencel in self-striping red, pink, and white. Each color change was clear and crisp, and I couldn't wait to get each stripe made. In the next three hours, I met dozens of new people, sold lots of books, and knitted almost to the heel of my delicious new candy-cane sock.

The beast was soothed, and the urge had passed. I

would survive. Even better, I'd have something to show for it.

I didn't need a cigarette.

I needed this kind of knitting magic, instead.

Our craft, with its particular alchemy, changes time and effort into something beautiful and useful, whereas smoking just changes clean lungs into dirty, damaged ones. At its core, smoking had never transformed me into a better anything, and when I used to tell myself it did—that it made me cooler, more confident, more likable—I was lying to myself. Knitting, on the other hand, transforms not only yarn into clothing, but knitters into calm, confident people who have a community of their own.

And, when necessary, we still have something to hide behind.

Ten Years Later
    I quit smoking when I was twenty-nine. I'm forty-nine now. Twenty years of not smoking, and I still wonder if I could have just one. I know I can't. So I haven't. And I won't. But if the world is ever given an expiration date—*the sun will explode in twenty-two hours!*—I'm driving to the nearest convenience store and taking all their cigarettes, using either cash or force. I will then smoke my way into a sweet, sweet nicotine oblivion. There. I said it.

WHIPSTITCH

The first Alice Starmore–designed sweater I ever saw was called Golden Gate, from her book *Pacific Coast Highway.* My friend Anne was wearing it and I had a difficult time focusing on the food on the table in front of me, or on Anne, who was visiting from out of town. Instead, I focused on the sweater's graceful, swooping cables, unable to take my eyes off the iron girders evoked by the pattern. Anne's sweater was the same rust red as the bridge, and I could almost smell the fog and hear the seagulls.

It was a piece of art—a warm, gorgeous representation of an architectural icon. It was incredible. I wanted it.

I've rarely experienced that level of covetousness in my life. If Anne had not been a friend, there's a possibility I would have entered a life of crime that morning, out in the parking lot. *Tourist robbed of sweater, left in waffle shop parking lot, shivering.*

But I refrained from robbery. I merely swallowed my jealousy with the last of my pancake and then, as I was unable to foot the three-hundred-dollar eBay charge for the out-of-print *Pacific Coast Highway* pattern book, I headed instead to my nearest knitting store and found Starmore's more recent *The Celtic Collection*.

I opened the book and tumbled headfirst into it. Cromarty, a boxy, intricately cabled pullover, grabbed me by the neck and shook me. In the pattern, the lanky redheaded model lounges on a rocky shoreline. Wild fiber lust filled my body. I had to have that sweater. Wearing it, I knew I'd inevitably end up spending a lot of time on a rugged coast too.

In the pattern description, Starmore mentions the incorporated Celtic crosses and the Pictish stones of Eastern Scotland. Pictish! I didn't even know what the word meant; I just knew I wanted to have something Pictish in my life. It sounded magical, as if the sweater itself would be casting runes for me. Who knew? Who cared? It would be mine.

I blogged about wanting to make the sweater, and Michigan's ThreadBear Fiber Arts offered to give me yarn if I knitted it as a shop model for their store. They'd display it for six months, and then they'd mail it back to me, a win-win situation. I agreed, and they sent me fifteen skeins of Koigu Kersti in a luscious variegated brown.

I sat down and picked up a US size four needle. I'm a loose knitter, after all. This was an important sweater—I was actually going to do a gauge swatch. I cast on. It didn't work. I went down to a three. Then a two. Now, gauge is a beast sometimes. I tried not to care that while swatching I couldn't get the right gauge in the DK-weight yarn until I went down to a US size one needle. It would be the same number of stitches, no matter how tiny the needle was, right? How hard could it be?

Answer: *so* hard. I was used to knitting projects that could be worked in loud, crowded bars without difficulty. Cromarty was *not* that kind of knitting. I had to pay attention to the chart at the beginning of every single row. I started to wonder if the ThreadBear boys had placed too much trust in me. Maybe I just wasn't a good enough knitter for this.

Ripping back, something that normally reduced me to fits of swearing, became old hat. Knitters gasped as I pulled out intricate inches of cable work. "No one will ever notice that mis-crossed cable," they told me, still pale from witnessing an hour of work unravel.

That had always been *my* line. I'd never understood why people needed their knitting to be perfect. People who reknitted sleeves because they didn't fit exactly right into the sleeve caps made my fingers twitch. Instead, I'd push and pull, jiggering pieces of sweaters until they finally looked approximately right. Of course, that meant that while I ended up with some great sweaters, others hung oddly from my shoulders, and my bind-offs were sometimes a bit wonky. But it would never be noticed from a trotting horse, I thought (not that I'm around many folks on trotting horses), and I was fine with that.

But not so for Cromarty. She had to be perfect. Since I was making her to be placed on display, I couldn't tolerate errors that I'd allow in other sweaters. When it eventually hung in the store, people would fondle it, pick it up, try it on, examine the seams. My name would be on it. I had a knitting blog. I wrote novels about knitting. I couldn't bear the thought of the knitting world finding me out as someone who couldn't knit a Starmore, and the nervousness was getting to me.

I thought about quitting and sending the yarn back.

What if I just couldn't do it? What it ended up only good as an around-the-house sweater, one that I'd wear while writing on cold afternoons when I knew I wouldn't see anyone else, taking the place of my ugly Cal Poly sweatshirt with its ketchup stain?

But quitting would mean that I'd failed. So when I'd discover a miscrossed cable, I'd ladder down to it, correcting it on my way back up. While doing that, I'd see another incorrect cable to the side of it, so I'd rip back six or eight more painful rows. Knitting back up, I'd inevitably find another error. The reverse side was always purl, so I'd rest on those rows, knowing the next row was pumping iron, getting ready to kick my ass.

I gave myself permission to cry whenever I had to rip more than ten rows at once. I'd never cried so much over a piece of knitting. If I wasn't actually on a rugged coastline, I was creating my own salt sea.

It was taking forever and the going was painful. But I tried to believe it wouldn't beat me. I'd abandoned sweaters in progress when bored with them, but I'd never quit a sweater because it was too difficult. And while not an astonishingly fast knitter, I'm usually pretty speedy. Three months into knitting Cromarty, I was only done with the sleeves, and I already felt as if I'd given my whole life over to the project. I couldn't think about anything else. I gave myself mini deadlines—knit to row 62 by midnight —and I'd race to make them, introducing even more errors as I went. What's more, every time I looked in the mirror I found more prematurely gray hairs, and I was pretty sure they were a direct result of Cromarty. I thought again about quitting but then rejected that idea as impossible. I was committed.

One night, as I drifted off to sleep thinking about the bottom hem of the back, I realized I was . . . perhaps a little obsessed. Okay, a lot obsessed. But where was the harm in that? I wasn't out drinking in every bar in town (though I did like to drink wine while knitting, something that might have led to a few crossed cables). I wasn't on drugs (at least not that often; it is California, after all). No, my true obsession was yarn, soft and squooshy. Who cared? I forged ahead, dreaming of being that redhead on the coastline in the Cromarty photograph.

When I was three-quarters of the way through the fifteen skeins the shop sent me, I had a feeling that I might be in very real trouble. I'd finished only the sleeves and part of the back. There was no way I'd have enough yarn, and the Koigu was hand dyed by small batch in Canada. The shop sent more to me in the same colorway but from a different dye lot. It was three shades lighter and completely unusable.

I sat in a corner gibbering for a little while. Cromarty was bigger to me now than just a display sweater, more than just a challenge. I wanted to *be* on those rugged coastal rocks already, dammit! Only I was becoming a little nervous that the shore in question was actually going to be the Cromarty Firth, the bay in northeastern Scotland in which, just before World War II, the Royal Navy laid out thirty miles of cable in order to detect and destroy German

U-boats. I felt as if I were swimming underwater laying the cables, the cables made of merino rather than steel. It was getting difficult to hold my breath.

Koigu asked for a sample of my remaining yarn, and I shipped it northward along with prayers for favorable winds and excellent dye-pot luck. They sent back ten new skeins that matched perfectly, for a total of twenty-five— my myriad cables gobbled the yardage, and I ended up using every single one.

When I sewed the sweater together and bound off at the neck, Cromarty was dense, as heavy as leather. With its gauge, though, the drape was lovelier than I could have predicted, and the intricacy of the cables was truly magnificent. It was a showstopper. I'd made it into the bay, safe and sound, and could finally come up for air. Now I had to find that coastline.

The finishing was strangely anticlimactic. There was no applause. Digit didn't care. I took a few pictures and then, with nothing else to do, I packed it into a box and sent it away. I fought silly tears. Would they take good enough care of her there? Would customers be too rough with her? I couldn't bear to think about it, so to get my mind off her, I cast on for a top-down raglan in heavy worsted wool. It felt like floating easily on my back after the underwater maneuvers I'd been performing, and I finished the simple stockinette sweater in two weeks.

Months later, when the box came back to me, I opened it carefully, reverentially. I lifted the sweater out, and even though it was a warm fall day, I layered it over a T-shirt, put the top down on my convertible, and drove across the Richmond Bridge to Dharma Trading in San Rafael. I didn't even feel like shopping—I just wanted someone else to see it and recognize it for what it was.

It worked. As if it had been scripted, the first woman I saw in the store let out a yelp when she saw me.

"Starmore!" she cried. "Which book?"

"*The Celtic Collection,*" I said, blushing furiously in pleasure.

"Cromarty." Another woman nodded. "I did that one too. Almost killed me."

"I did this on size ones," I said, unable to hide the pride in my voice.

The gasps were audible.

And there, surrounded by people who spoke my language, I was finally proud of myself. I'd done it. I'd made the sweater of my dreams, and I loved the way the accomplishment felt on my shoulders.

On my way home that day, I drove out to the Albany Bulb. The scrubby little outcropping of land juts into the San Francisco Bay and is populated only by wandering artists and people walking their dogs. As I walked in the wind, I considered the Pictish cables I was wearing. I'd researched them, finally, and learned that Alice Starmore had been inspired by the patterns for them from a stone from the late eighth century, found in a churchyard in Nigg on the Cromarty Firth where, twelve hundred years later, the miles and miles of cable would be laid underwater. Across the water from me, I grinned at the cables of the Golden Gate Bridge—each cable made of twenty-seven thousand strands of wire twisted around each other. For me, this sweater was my Golden Gate. It was my ridiculous challenge, accomplished.

I wore Cromarty on the rugged coastline and knew I was finally the knitter I wanted to be.

*T*en Years Later
Okay, so I hate to break it to you, but I really should. I wore that sweater only once or twice after that trip to the bay. It was just *too* boxy. *Too* dense. It sat folded neatly in my closet until about a week ago, when I finally gave it to my sister with strict orders for her to give it to a thrift store if she doesn't wear it. She swears she *will* wear it, and she lives directly on the coast overlooking the Pigeon Point lighthouse, so there's still hope for the rugged coastline to be part of Cromarty's journey.

You can see Cromarty, and a lot of my other knits, at my Ravelry page at ravelry.com/people/rachaelherron.

TREE OF LIFE

I wish I could show you the invisible lines of strata in my knitted socks—where I was and what was happening when each inch was made. After all these years knitting, though, my stitches are generally pretty even, so it's impossible to know exactly where I was when I made which stitches. But if suddenly the lines of time were somehow made visible on my sock-in-progress, I'd show you that here, at the toe, you'd see I was home on the couch, my border collie, Clara, at my side. Two inches up, I was waiting in line at the post office when a bouncing child joggled my arm before wanting a demonstration of what I was doing. When I turned the heel, I was at a funeral and used the completed toe to dry my eyes, and this long, straight section of ankle—right here—was done at work. Yep, I get to knit at work, making me one of the luckiest people alive. I work 911 dispatch, which can be a wonderful, frustrating, sometimes frightening job, and believe me when I say that stress-management tools are necessary for the profession. Knitting fits the bill.

Some of the rows in this sock were knitted while I was thinking about the man who accidentally dropped his child down a flight of stairs. The ones just above it were knitted while I worried about the forty-three-year-old woman who was transported to the hospital after a seizure, unconscious and barely breathing. Who would be there when she woke up? Did she have someone to hold her hand? I'm not often one for prayer, but I do wish for things. Those wishes get tangled in my stitches until the item itself feels like more than just a piece of fabric.

Not all my rows are complicated with emotion. Some of the knitting I do at work is relaxed, the stitches smooth and even. If I could point them out, I'd show you where I was knitting with my brain turned off, passing time between 911 calls and radio transmissions.

There are many myths about 911, but the most widely held myth is that all dispatchers sit together in one big room sharing a great pool of knowledge, and that they can control events and safety with a flick of the switch. They know, instantly, how big an earthquake is or when the power will be restored to your area. If you call 911 for your aunt who lives in another state who was having difficulty breathing while she was on the phone with you, the dispatcher will be able to transfer you quickly to the right agency.

Wrong.

While these are nice ideas, 911 isn't like that. In your town, there's a good chance you have at least a couple of different dispatch centers that you might get patched through to on a bad day (no one calls 911 because she's having a great day and wants to share). In many cities, including mine, police and fire are dispatched separately—the police agency is the primary answering point, and if the PD dispatcher decides your call needs fire or medical help, she transfers you to a center with specially trained dispatchers, like mine. And if you call for someone far away, chances are the dispatcher is going to have to Google the department's phone number to transfer you.

I've been a dispatcher for twelve years, and I think it's one of the best jobs in the world. On any given shift, I actually get to help—I give instructions to the woman whose husband has just passed out, or to the parent whose child is choking on a piece of carrot. I tell people how to do CPR. I instruct people how to deliver babies and how to tie off the umbilical cord. It's not a job that involves a lot of paper pushing—it's a job that requires you to be able to multitask and prioritize while real lives hang in the balance.

It sounds exciting, and it is. My jurisdiction has forty-nine fire stations and serves almost half a million people. In the fall, when the rains start and cars skid off the roads, we're busy dispatching engines and ambulances to traffic collisions. In winter, when people first start their fireplaces and propane heaters, structure fires abound. Spring brings ATV accidents, and summer brings vegetation fires that get measurably worse every year. And always, everywhere, people need medical help.

But it's another myth that 911 is *always* busy. Even in the biggest centers, there are down times. Dispatchers aren't paid to dust or clean or perform market research—they're paid to know what to do and whom to dispatch when the plane goes down or when the gas line explodes.

When it's quiet, though—unlike firefighters, who have

sleep time built into their shifts—dispatchers are paid to stay awake, which can be difficult in the middle of a silent night. Some read books, some chat with coworkers, some watch TV if their center allows it.

Many dispatchers knit.

To me, knitting is perfectly suited to the job. Knitting is typically portable, and once the knitter is proficient, the work can be dropped instantaneously in the lap when the call comes in. When the knitter isn't proficient, she learns to accept imperfections, because stitches will jump when she does, as she catches the phone on its first ring.

Many of the twenty-five dispatchers at my agency knit. My favorite knitting coworker, Cristian, is one of the toughest guys I know. A young veteran who lost his legs—one below the hip, one at the knee—in Iraq, Cris walks with two prosthetic devices, and sometimes the pain of walking on them makes him scowl. But he moves deliberately, his Humvee backpack slung across his shoulders. He never complains, which is astonishing to me. I whine if I get a paper cut. He tries not to drink much water during our long shifts, so that he doesn't have to make the walk to the bathroom often—I call him the camel and nag him to drink more water—and sometimes when his leg battery is low it beeps softly, like a dying cell phone.

Jim, another macho knitting coworker, taught Cris to knit during one night shift. "I showed him the basics," said Jim, "but then he just picked up the rest of it on his own." I have a photograph of Cris hunched over his needles in front of the dispatch console. He was frowning, eyes intense, and if someone gave me that look in a dark alley,

I'd run the other way. But he was busy making his wife a scarf in the Oakland Raiders colors: silver and black.

One morning, just after I'd heard he was knitting, I passed him on the walkway—I was leaving work, and he was coming on shift. He stopped me with a jerk of his head. "Hey."

"Yeah?" I was sleepy, ready to head home.

"I got this problem."

"You do?" I was surprised. Was he mad at a coworker? Was he mad at me? Had he had a bad call and needed to process it?

He paused and then looked up and down the ramp, making sure the coast was clear. In a low tone, he said hurriedly, "If I want to use two strands at once, do I have to get two different balls of yarn?"

I knew he wouldn't appreciate either the grin or the hug I wanted to give him, so I just said, "You can knit from both ends of the ball at once."

His eyes widened. "The inside and the outside tail."

"It'll tangle a little, but you can handle it." I'd assumed he'd just been fooling around with the needles, bored during the night. I'd never thought he would be one to wonder about technique, to do more than just garter stitch.

"Yeah," he said, with another tilt of his head. His voice was gruff. "Hey, thanks."

"Any time."

Cris is busy with his wife and two kids at home, and I know that in his downtime he likes to play video games, watch shoot'em-up movies, and buy Oakland A's bobble-heads on eBay. He may not be the typical candidate to get caught up in knit and purl. But his stitches are tight and even, and the scarves he turns out are lovely. All of the women in his life clamor for his creations.

I asked him once what he liked about knitting. He shrugged and said, "Just something to do, I guess. It passes the time."

"You're really good at it," I said.

"I only make scarves."

"That's something," I said, and I meant it.

At work, we sit in our chairs for twelve to eighteen hours at a stretch. Our breaks are taken at our terminals. For some of us, knitting in our downtime is our break. When the phone rings, we all drop our work in our laps and race each other to help someone who's scared and in pain. I can't tell from looking at my knitting who called us when; I can't see the places where I was stressed out as opposed to whiling wee hours away.

I bet Cris's knitting is the same way. I'm sure that when Cris's wife, Blanca, wears her scarf, she doesn't think about the people her husband talked to, the way his voice got softer when the caller started crying, the way he just picked up his work afterward and added more even, deliberate stitches. I wonder if he ever considers the energy he's bringing to the work through his hands, but I'm a little too shy to ask. I think it's something beautiful and rare, a tough young veteran like him performing a traditional craft, and I don't want to scare or embarrass him into quitting by asking something like, "Do you put wishes into your knitting?" Perhaps he's never considered the invisible lines that run through his knitting, like they do mine.

But I consider those lines. And now I see them in other places too. In the carefully placed blueberries on top of my locally made muffin: what was the baker thinking about when she made it? Will I taste a difference if she was worried about her ailing grandmother or dreaming about her boyfriend? Or what about the way my mail carrier delivers mail on my street? I'll never be able to tell what emotions he carried as he dropped the circulars into my box, but I can guarantee this: he had emotion then, about something, and if he was worried about the argument he'd had that morning with his partner, I hope the act of clicking my mailbox shut and latching my gate acts for him as a kind of mechanical prayer. From the way I've felt yarn slipping through my fingers, I've learned that rote work, like dropping mail into boxes or placing blueberries onto muffins or knitting garter stitch with bamboo needles, can be more than just an act.

Each tiny action can be a wish, a dream, a desire, all of these tangled together in what usually comes down to a distillation of one thing: *hope*.

Ten Years Later
It's been more than five years since I became a full-time writer, and there isn't a single day that I don't think about the dispatchers working in every city and town around the globe. At this very second, they're ready for a call I hope you never have to make. Every time I hear a siren, I think about the person who talked to the caller and about the person telling the responding unit where to go and what to do once they get there.

I once lost five people in a row during the first hour of my shift—four failed CPR attempts on adults followed by a failed CPR attempt on a baby. That was the only time I can remember wanting to go home early from a shift, but of course, I didn't. I just kept answering calls. That's what we always did, no matter how hard the day got. Dispatchers are the first first-responders, and they're often completely forgotten when it comes to debriefs and peer support, but they never quit doing their job until their relief is standing behind their chair, ready to plug in and take over where they left off.

So, if you're a dispatcher, I say this from my heart, *thank you* for what you do. I see you.

And if you don't know a dispatcher, why not surprise a communications center near you with a Starbucks run and a dozen donuts? Tell them I sent you. Oh, and make sure you admire their knitting, too.

PICK UP AND KNIT

*K*nitters often joke about the Sweater Curse, but most take the superstition more seriously than they'd like to admit—they tend to knock wood after laughing. The idea is that if a knitter makes a sweater for a boyfriend, the relationship is doomed. In a variation of the myth, the relationship might even end while the sweater is still on the needles. In any form, knitting a sweater for a boyfriend (not a husband—they're exempt) guarantees a breakup, and the knitter is said to have fallen prey to the Sweater Curse.

No one knows who first told the story—is it an old wives' tale? Did some guy somewhere just freak out when receiving such a strong evidence of love? Why doesn't the break-up rule apply to other acts of love, like mending clothes, or picking the loved one up at the airport, or the ill-advised action of getting the significant other's name in tattoo form? No matter where the legend came from, it lives on in the collective consciousness of knitters everywhere, and many knitters consider it before buying that gorgeous dark blue yarn that would go so well with his dreamy eyes.

I never worried about the myth. For a long time, I dated only men, and I'd never considered knitting any of them a sweater. Perhaps it was what they wore that discouraged my craft: Roger wore polar fleece or tank tops, Luis wore tattered sweaters from JCPenney, and Mick never wore more than a tee-shirt, no matter the weather. None of them were great at laundry, and I didn't trust them not to ruin a hand-knit sweater. So I never gave the curse any thought.

Then, for a while, I dated both men and women. Those were heady, busy days of falling in love every six or seven months, and, honestly, I was too preoccupied to knit much of anything, even for myself.

After a while, I met Jenn. My first long-term girlfriend, she was the first significant other I thought might be worthy of my knitting time. I briefly considered the Sweater Curse, but since it was often called the Boyfriend's Sweater Curse, I decided it wouldn't apply to this situation.

When I brought the idea up, we were sitting on the back porch of a hotel room in Mendocino. It was an idyllic scene: big wooden chairs on the dark wood balcony, green cliff below us dropping away down to the crashing blue waters of the Pacific. Gulls wheeled above us.

"What if I knitted you a sweater?" I said.

Jenn was absorbed in her book and didn't look up. "I think you should."

Somehow, it didn't seem like a big enough reaction. "Hmmm."

"You fly, I'll buy," she said.

Well. *That* was enough.

We found a yarn store in Fort Bragg, a small town just north of Mendocino, and Jenn chose a pretty heathered purple merino. I picked out a simple raglan pattern and cast on that afternoon, sitting again on the dark wooden chair. Jenn retreated inside when the fog rolled in, but I stayed out there, knitting in the heavy, wet mist, listening to the foghorn.

The sweater turned out perfectly. It was a good fit, and the light purple was a great color with her dark brown hair. Jenn loved it.

Then we broke up.

The separation was mutual. It wasn't working for either of us, and it was better for us to part. But I wondered about the curse—was it the sweater's fault? Did that last stitch clinch it? Was it because the hem rolled up that our connection was severed?

Although tempting, I didn't blame the sweater as much as I blamed my desire to be alone and autonomous. And besides, we were women. It didn't apply, right? But just as I throw spilled salt over my left shoulder and never open umbrellas indoors, I resolved I wouldn't knit another girl-friend a sweater.

That was fine. It meant I got to keep all my knitting.

After a short time-out, I licked my wounds and got back into the dating pool, sans needles. I joined a couple of internet dating sites, and I loved pouring myself a glass of wine or two on Friday nights and cruising the listings. It was astonishing how quickly I could fall in love with an online profile—a few witty back-and-forth emails and I had the whole relationship planned.

Then we'd meet. I'd be disappointed when the person who said she was a thrill-seeker turned out to be a timid accountant who wouldn't drive a mile over the speed limit, or the one who said she valued creative expression thought Thomas Kinkade puzzles were the height of fine art. I exchanged a volley of email with a doctor at the local children's hospital, and, by our correspondence, I knew we were perfect together. I imagined our Christmas cards, a dog posed at our feet wearing a Santa hat. I knew there was absolutely no chemistry five minutes into our first date. At all. She could have stepped on my toe and I probably wouldn't have felt it. Then I dated a writer who was sexy and smart, and we *did* have chemistry, but when it came to dinner dialogue, the repartee we found so easy online fell flat.

One woman caught my eye even though by then I was getting tired of the internet routine. Her profile showed her crouched in front of a velvet Elvis painting, her smile wickedly pleased with something just to the right of the camera's lens. I read her profile five times. She was quirky, down to earth, funny. Some of the lines in her profile were so perfect they made me ache.

But I didn't contact her. Instead, I started a knitting circle at the local gay bar that was just blocks from my house. I advertised it on Craigslist, and I walked to the first afternoon session surprisingly nervous. What if no one came and I ended up knitting alone? What if, and this was worse, only one person came, and I had to make polite chitchat for the next two hours with someone who liked to crochet tiny pineapples?

I was thrilled when fifteen women showed up. This was

back when knitting in public was something people didn't see very often. When perhaps eight or ten people were already gathered around the tables, staring at our work in the dimness of the bar, another woman joined us. She said, "You're the knitters. Obviously."

"Yep," I said.

She threw a bag of knitting onto the table. "Can someone *please* help me finish this hat? I can't figure out the decreases, and I'm going to rip it into pieces if I don't figure it out soon."

It was her, the woman from the Elvis painting. My heart raced. This was a sign, it had to be. And sure enough, at the end of the knit-out, Toni followed me outside, grinning that wicked smile.

"Do you like baseball?" she asked.

"Nope," I said. "But I'll go anyway."

After a few very promising dates, as my heart dipped its toes into the waters of infatuation, I wanted to make something for her. Certainly not anything like a sweater, but I thought a striped scarf might be nice. Just a little token of the depth of emotion I knew we were both beginning to feel.

I finished it and tucked it into my bag, ready to give to her. We were staying in her family's house in Montara Beach, and we walked down to the water. Night had already descended, and the paths through the ice plant at the sandy edge were lit up by moonlight. Where the dry sand turned to wet, Toni turned to face me. "I can't do this." Then she started to cry. I was tough and got all the way back to my car before my own tears started. I used the stupid scarf to dry my face and wrapped it around my neck for the drive back home, making it mine again. It was soaked by the time I got back to Oakland.

I stopped responding to ads, took down my profile, and stopped internet dating. All my crushes, fanned into virtual flame, died quickly in person. It wasn't worth it. I was officially done with dating, and certainly done with knitting for anyone that wasn't related to me by blood. I stopped going to the knitting group I'd started at the gay bar and went back to knitting alone, on my couch. I'd be a little old cat lady, and I was happy about it.

I swear I didn't mean to see Lala's online profile. It was, mostly, accidental. Admitting this feels really dumb, but this is true: I was reading *Salon.com* and noticed they had personals. I assumed they wouldn't have women-for-women personals, and I clicked the link to prove it to myself—so I could what? So I could complain to them about it? I've never been sure what I was planning on doing. But they did, of course, have gay personals, and I proved it to myself by clicking on just *one* of them.

Lala lived in Oakland, played the banjo, and she knitted. A bluegrass-playing knitter in my town? How was that possible? I wrote her a short message: "Do I know you? Because if I don't, I should. I'm not dating, nor am I interested in dating, but if you'd like to get a beer sometime, that would be fun."

We met at a bar. She was an hour and a half late, but she had a good excuse, and I had my knitting, so I didn't mind. It wasn't a date, after all. We talked for hours. I admitted that I was a runner—she was horrified—and she admitted that she was widowed, her young wife, Aura, having died of melanoma a few years prior. I couldn't even begin to

imagine what that had been like. We met two more times—
I wasn't sure if they were dates or if we even had chemistry, but I tried not to think about it. On our fourth date, she picked up the banjo and played it, her hands deft and sure. I kissed her then, the banjo still between us.

True love hit me like a bus. I knew within three months that I wanted to spend the rest of my life with her.

She wasn't getting a sweater, though. Not on my watch. I knew that much. I knitted her fingerless gloves, decorated with a banjo on one hand, and *La* on the other. She worked in a chilly office and loved the warmth of the red alpaca I used.

Six months into the best relationship I'd ever had, my resolve starting to crumble, I was dying to buy some yarn and knit love into the stitches that would wrap all the way around her. But I wouldn't do it. I'd gotten lucky with the gloves so far—we hadn't had so much as an argument since I'd given them to her.

She wanted a sweater though. "Please? The curse doesn't count if there's no boyfriend involved." She was a knitter—she knew what I was worried about.

"Nope." I sat on the couch in her apartment.

"Just a small one. I'm not that big."

"No way. I'm not risking losing you," I cuddled Harriet, the dog she'd brought into my life.

"What would it take for you to make me one?"

I laughed. "A ring, probably." I was totally kidding. I never planned on getting married—it wasn't on any check-off list I'd ever made for my life.

"Okay, then."

I looked at her. She sounded serious. "Excuse me?"

"Maybe someday." She kissed me.

I stammered and tried to pretend we'd never had this conversation, but one night as we stood in my kitchen, indulging in late-night kitchen cocktails after her band played a show, we just knew. "Married," I murmured, looking at my naked left hand. "Really?"

"Really," she said into my neck. "I can't not marry you."

And somehow, I felt the same way.

In the morning, we both woke up so hungover our teeth hurt. I mumbled, "Did we…?"

She put a hand to her head. "Coffee first."

After the coffee kicked in, we both admitted that yes, even in the sober light of day, we wanted to *marry* each other. We were astonished, ecstatic, and terrified.

We told no one for months, hiding the actual engagement rings that we bought. I made myself a sweater instead. I used tan and pink cheap wool from Michael's—I wanted it in a hurry—and made a raglan striped pullover. The only thing special about it was that I had added a band of pink hearts in one of the tan stripes around the left wrist. I thought of it as my engagement sweater, a secret ring that only she and I knew about.

After I finished knitting my secret sweater?

I took a deep breath and looked at my engagement ring. We were almost ready to come out with the secret to our families. We'd started making actual plans for the illegal ceremony, the one that wouldn't make us married in any *legal* way because it was illegal in both our state and our country, but we still wanted to say the words to each other.

If something dumb like the Sweater Curse could break

us up, I needed to know now that we weren't meant for each other, rather than later.

So I bought yarn for her first sweater, sturdy gray wool that had a deep blue undertone. Night after night, I knitted it into a sweater that echoed a western shirt, with plackets and brass old-west stars for buttons. When she put it on, she grinned so big she could have lit up Las Vegas.

Reader, I married her.

Seven years and three weddings later (two legal, in two different countries), she has enough sweaters to carry her through the coldest winter our Northern California climate can throw at her. Now she has a green cabled sweater and a rugged gray one. She has one made from an old Mary Maxim pattern, with two country dancers on the back. I will state for the record: intarsia equals love, period. But I think my favorite one I've made her is the one with the Space Invader on the lower right front—it's just right, so her.

So it seems that true love really does conquer all. It conquers petty arguments over vacuuming, financial troubles requiring meals made of lentils, and dismal choices regarding driving routes. The Sweater Curse—boyfriend or not—is no match for a love that sees past the stitches, even the occasional dropped one, into the heart.

Ten Years Later

When the first edition of this book came out, I got quite a few grumbles about the "political" content I included around queerness. Now, I believe that writers must be political—it's part of our job. But although the *legality* of one's sexual orientation is often quite literally political, the fact of one's orientation is not, just like having brown eyes isn't, either. It's just a simple fact. So I cheerfully ignored all the complaints and bad reviews from people who felt I was pushing a gay agenda upon them. Look, if you don't agree with gay marriage, please don't have one. It's that simple.

However, I did get an email that completely rocked me. It was from a woman who wrote an Amazon review that said she'd gotten to this chapter, the one you just read, and had to stop reading in disgust. She'd been loving the book up to that point, she said, but she felt I'd "tricked" her into reading gay content. She said she'd burn it if she could, but she didn't believe in burning books, so she'd be donating it to the library.

I never saw the review—what I saw was her follow-up email to me saying she'd *deleted* the review, and here was why:

"I really did want to burn your book, and I was so mad at you for tricking me into reading a gay book. I set your book on my coffee table and I walked away. But the next day, I couldn't stand it, I had to know what happened next, so I kept reading, even though I was really mad at myself for doing it. You changed my mind, Rachael. I never knew a gay person before now. People on the TV don't count, not like this. Your book helped me realize that you're just a normal person, just like me. I'm sorry for being so closed-minded for so long. Just thought you should know you changed someone's mind."

Y'all.

The *joy* I felt at reading this. I never, ever set out to

convince someone that being any flavor of LGBTQIA was an okay thing to be, because first, I think changing people's opinions is hard to do, especially with hot-button topics, and second, honey, I don't have the *time.* But the fact that it happened? At least once?

Wow.

Just, *wow.*

KNIT TWO TOGETHER

*W*hen I got engaged, I developed the romantic notion that I'd knit my own wedding dress. I envisioned myself in a simple knitted bodice with lace inserts, attached to a lace-edged skirt. Wedding guests would be gobsmacked by the dress's beauty and elegance. I had it all planned out, which was surprising, coming from me.

I was never a girl who dreamed about her ideal wedding. I didn't have a hope chest, and I didn't practice that step-together-step walk that other girls did when playing with their mothers' veils. When I was six or seven, I very clearly remember making a decision: when I was really old (twenty or so), I would have lots of boyfriends but I'd live with my favorite girl. Whether that was prophetic, or coincidental, or I knew then that I was bi, it didn't change the fact that I'd never imagined a white wedding for myself.

But now that I was engaged, I wanted to make something gorgeous, something that I loved, something that would look great on me, with my own two hands. My engagement sweater was nice, with its knitted hearts circling the left wrist, but it wasn't even close to being a showstopper. A knitted wedding gown—yeah, that would be something.

Friends thought I was banana-pants. "Why would you work so hard for something you'll only ever wear once?"

Eh. What did they know? They weren't knitters. Okay, some of them were, but I discounted their opinions just as readily. They weren't thinking about it the right way—they weren't imagining the joy of creating something gorgeous that would probably end up being a family heirloom, passed down through generations. I imagined carefully boxing the dress away after the wedding, wrapping it in acid-free tissue paper, storing it carefully with cedar chips to keep it safe and moth-free. Years hence, maybe I'd bring it out for a cherished great-niece who would be so overwhelmed by the heritage of the stitches that she'd knit her own matching shawl to go with it.

Big dreams.

They lasted until I started trying to find a pattern. I did online searches, and I was surprised to find that many people had already held knitted weddings. What? I wasn't the first knitting-mad person to fall in love? I suppose I could have predicted that result, given the popularity of knitting, but I was surprised at how *many* there were, the vast majority of them absolutely awful. I found online photos of women wearing gowns that made them look like frosted doilies, grooms standing at attention with crocheted bow ties and cummerbunds made of yarn. The attendants held pom-pom flowers. Frankly, the online galleries freaked me out.

Every single pattern I found was nothing short of hideous. I didn't want my dress to look like a Halloween costume—I didn't want anyone laughing at me if they found me on the internet.

My fiancée, Lala, asked me, "What are you trying to prove?" She wasn't against the idea—far from it—but she was honestly curious.

"I don't need to prove anything. I just want a beautiful dress for our day, and the most beautiful thing to me is knitting."

"Well," she said in her reassuring Lala way, "you'll be the most beautiful thing there. I don't care if you wear sweatpants."

But the more I thought about it, I realized I was trying to prove a point—I wanted to be the girl who knitted her own dress and pulled it off beautifully. My hubris chastened me when I recognized it, and I finally scaled down my idea.

I found an Edwardian-looking bodice in a knitting magazine. I could wear it again, I thought, on a gorgeous spring morning somewhere, remembering my wedding day. And I found the skirt of my dreams in another magazine, lace edged and delicate. I'd line it and wear that again, too, with tank tops and cute shoes. That wouldn't be too show-offy, would it?

Together, the pieces, knitted in the softest pale yellow, would make me look like a 1920s bride. I would find a charming hat to perch askew on the curls that would be created for the day.

I could see it all. It was going to be perfect.

I had four months before the big day. Plenty of time. I'd make the skirt first, I thought. Lovely miles of stockinette intersected by trails of lace working downward. I cast on in excitement . . . which wore off by round twelve. Holy hell, there were a lot of stitches. And such a fine gauge! I never knitted to this kind of gauge, and my shoulders and neck started to hurt from looking down all the time, poring over the small stitches. The pain was new and unwelcome.

The more that people expressed surprise (and thinly veiled dismay) that I was knitting my own wedding clothes, the more stubborn I became. I knitted faster. I brought the skirt with me to work and I knitted when it was quiet. I knitted all the time.

Finally, it was done. Holding it up, I knew it was perfect. Lovely and light, it would cling to my hips and hang just past my knees, curving exactly the way I'd wanted.

Then I tried it on and looked at myself in the mirror.

I burst into tears.

I wanted to feel beautiful and elegant, but this skirt looked home-damn-made. Instead of draping seductively from my curves, it clung to my belly, showcasing it, and then hung loosely to my knees. And I hadn't even started working on the bodice yet.

I didn't show Lala the skirt, but I told her about it.

"Then just buy something," she said.

Easy for her to say; we'd found an incredible ivory suit for her, along with a black shirt with sequins on the collar.

She was going to look like a million bucks. I was going to look like forty-two cents.

"What about a whatchamacallit?" I asked. "A girdle? Maybe I can go to Macy's and get some Spanx. Isn't everyone supposed to have one of those? Do you think it'll disguise my belly?"

Lala shot me a look over her coffee cup, the mug with the heat-sensitive cow that disappears when filled with hot liquid. "I don't care. It's not about the clothes." Her tone was firm. She meant it. Something about the way she said it finally shook me out of my bridal daze, and I heard what she didn't say out loud: she'd been married before. She'd already walked down one aisle toward Aura, the love of her life—she'd already done all the cake tasting and invitation picking. What she cared about, now, was me, the second love of her life, something she'd never thought she'd find.

I glanced in the full-length mirror I'd propped in the dining room in order to look at the skirt: I was wearing sweats and an old beat-up T-shirt. My hair stuck up in places and lay flat in others. Not a stitch of makeup, not even lipstick, which I never left the house without.

She loved me like this. I was being a drama queen, and she still loved me.

Finally, I got it. It *didn't* matter what I wore. What mattered was who I was walking toward, not what I was wearing when I walked. It wasn't about me—it was about us.

I ended up going to Macy's, and I found a dress on the sale rack. It was inexpensive for a dress of its style, probably designed for a society woman to wear to a fancy dinner. A cream sheath with beads and sequins, it had spaghetti straps, a low bodice, and hugged perfectly every curve while disguising the ones I wanted hidden. At the knee, it flared out into a flurry of silk and net. It was being sold as a fancy cocktail frock.

But on me, it was my wedding dress, because in it, I was going to marry Lala.

I still wanted to knit something, of course, because I don't give up that easily. I only had a month left. I cast on for a shawl in cream Cascade Indulgence, something I'd had in my yarn stash for years. I designed a lace pattern with the help of Barbara Walker's books, and I knitted the lace faster than I ever have before or since. It felt like riding the knitting rapids. I knew I would get it done in time, though it would be close. But I knitted with a different intention: I was making the shawl to honor our day, in order to make a keepsake that would hold sentiment and memory. I wasn't just knitting it for me.

I finished the shawl. And as I walked down the aisle (bare armed, because after all that, I forgot to put the shawl on until the very end of the reception), I felt like the most beautiful woman in the world, the way every woman should feel on her wedding day.

Even though neither of us are Jewish, the shawl felt like a kind of chuppah, a wedding canopy. A cloth held over the heads of two people getting married, sometimes it's fancy, stretched over four poles, and sometimes it's a simple tallis, a prayer shawl usually made of wool and held up by friends' hands. Using a chuppah in the ceremony symbolizes "home," and spiritually it means that God blesses the covenant of marriage. It represented our creating a home together, a family newly composed of the two of us. Every step I'd been taking with Lala had brought us to this place. I was leaving my single life and entering a shared one.

I've only worn the shawl once since then, to a lovely wedding where it shed white alpaca fiber onto the dark suits of every man I hugged. It's usually folded on one of my sweater shelves. But I run my fingers over it from time to time, and I remember the promises we made and think about the home we've built.

Together.

Ten Years Later
In case you're wondering what a *real* knitted wedding dress looks like, go look at my friend Stephanie's wedding dress. You'll be stunned. She designed it, too. See it here: rachaelherron.com/stephanie (Ravelry link).

And this: my mother's wedding gift to me was the hope chest I'd never had or even knew I wanted. I loved it instantly—the cedar smell reminded me of the scent of her hope chest, in which she'd always stored her knitting patterns and extra yarn. Cedar smells like safety.

Lala and I are moving to New Zealand, and that chest is the only piece of furniture that's coming with us. Tucked away inside is my wedding shawl. But the thing that matters most won't be in the chest—the thing that matters most is Lala's hand in mine as we move forward into a new life.

BASKET WEAVE STITCH

For many years, my cat, Digit, and my knitting were the only two constants in my life. I moved all over Oakland, and in every new place, he'd go outside, kick ass and take names, and come home at night to recover, pressed against me as I knitted. I developed a special whistle that would bring him running to me from a block away. I changed jobs, but he stuck around. I dated, and he gave only a select few a second glance—those were the ones I gave a third glance.

Before Digit came into my life, I hadn't planned on being a cat lady. You know the stereotype: the woman who knits and lies in bed eating bonbons and reading romance novels. I already had the knitting and the fondness for romance novels—I didn't need another strike.

Nevertheless, I did want a cat. My boyfriend at the time was completely against it. He was allergic, and if we were going to end up living together, he said a cat was out of the question. Naturally, that just made me want one more. Instead, for Christmas he got me a Tamagotchi, a little electronic pet that was popular in 1997. It required constant care, and I'd killed it by New Year's Eve. He was pleased and thought it should prove something to me. What it proved was that a plastic keychain toy was totally inadequate when it came to cuddling, and that he was an ass.

So I was completely ready, when my upstairs neighbors came down to my apartment with two tiny kittens, to take the plunge. Not yet weaned, perhaps only four or five weeks old, the kittens had to be fed by dipping pieces of cloth into formula for them to suck. They wobbled when they tried to walk, their legs giving out unexpectedly from beneath them.

It was love at first bite. The instant he sank his tiny little milk teeth into my hand, the second I laid eyes on the extra toes that made up those huge feet of his, I was hooked. The woman who'd brought the kittens down to show me also wanted one, and I felt a fierce urge to scoop up "my" kitten and run. The other cat looked almost exactly like Digit, except he wasn't a polydactyl, and instead of wanting to box and nip, he wanted to curl and cuddle. My neighbor petted the quiet one who was yawning in her lap seductively. "I like this calm one," she said. The relief was overwhelming, and I didn't know how to say thank you. I wasn't good at asking for things, and I was worse at receiving them. I didn't know how to say that I wanted, *needed* this cat.

We belonged to each other instantly. I know. I can see your eye roll from here and I don't blame you. But it's the simple truth: I was now a cat lady.

As Digit grew, his natural tendency toward violent

exuberance didn't abate. His favorite game was to shred whatever I was knitting, but he only attacked if it was moving in my hands. He loved to get under the sheets when I made the bed and then growl and claw me through the fabric as I patted his rear end. Or he'd jump into an empty laundry basket so I could swing it around and around, the force of gravity keeping him in it as he purred like a freight train, refusing to get out when I wanted to use the basket for more prosaic things, like laundry. He howled without ceasing if I didn't let him outside at exactly the moment he wanted to go, and followed up the howling by peeing in inappropriate places in retaliation for my slowness. I got good at running to do his bidding. Finally, I built a two-by-four ramp up to my window so he could come in and out at will, and he did, bringing various half-dead birds and snakes in with him, usually when I was sleeping (there's nothing like a bloody bird flapping itself against the kitchen windows to wake a person up).

When Digit did manage to sleep with me, he curled at my head, next to my pillow. What he most wanted to do was to suck on the neck of my shirt, but I broke him of the habit by holding his paw, letting him nuzzle my hand. When I rolled over, he'd get up with a sigh and thump over me with his huge feet so he could settle next to my head again, and put his paw in my hand.

It's said that the internet is made up of three categories: knitting, porn, and pictures of cute animals. I can vouch for two of the three. The knitters who visited my blog loved Digit. Sometimes I got more comments on pictures of him than I did when I finished new sweaters, and if too much time passed without a photo of him, he got email from fans, wondering how he was doing.

Digit was my guy. He was the most important.

Then I met Lala. And she had dogs.

Falling in love with Harriet and Miss Idaho was part of the fun of being with Lala. Digit, though, wasted no time on such feelings. The way he hated the dogs, fueled by the gasoline from his overfull hate tank, was rivaled only by the way he loved me from the much smaller love tank he kept in a secret place right next to his furious spleen. After some time, he could grudgingly be in the same room with the dogs, but he still struck viciously at them whenever they got within range. They quickly learned to steer clear of the demon from hell.

Lala and I bought our home in East Oakland and moved the pack in. Digit roamed widely but came home with fewer trophies—there were more stray cats in our new neighborhood, and I think the pickings were slim when it came to rodents and birds.

One night in February, he didn't come home. I gave the whistle and didn't hear him thumping toward me. I tried several times that night to call him in, and he didn't come. I didn't worry too much. He'd been gone before, sometimes for a few days, always returning with patches of missing fur and an occasional claw from another cat shockingly stuck in his ornery hide, but otherwise just fine.

But he didn't come back. A week later, I started to cry. Two weeks later, I mourned. The space by my head seemed so cold and my hand felt empty when I slept. I felt too sad to knit anything but socks. I searched the streets, and I checked all the shelters, flipping through their heart-breaking kill files and peering into each cage. I put up fliers and offered rewards. I stopped when I drove past cats that had been recently killed by cars and moved their bodies up to the sidewalks, knowing that if it were Digit, I'd want someone to do the same for me. Maybe they'd find their pets and get to bury them. I hadn't been able to do that for Digit, and I grieved.

After about a month, I was finally able to write about it on my blog. I got dozens of condolence emails, stories of special cats and the people who loved them, and each email rebroke my heart. I didn't know how to thank anyone, not appropriately, not with the thanks they deserved, so I didn't respond to most of the emails—I just let their kind words wash over me.

Four months after Digit disappeared, I was sound asleep when Lala burst into our bedroom. She said, "You have to come to the kitchen. Now."

"Fire? *Fire?*" Crap. I'd been meaning to buy a fire extinguisher but hadn't gotten around to it yet.

"Nothing is wrong, but you need to come right *now.*"

"I swear to God," I mumbled, "if this is a picture on Cute Overload, I will kill you."

"Just *move.*"

In the kitchen, square in the middle of the tiled floor, sat Digit, swaying as if he were drunk. Wait, *was* this Digit? He'd been a sixteen-pound bruiser; this cat couldn't have been more than seven or eight pounds. His face was swollen and I wasn't sure his left eye was intact. His entire rear end was a mass of infection, and he stank to high heaven. Lala said that she'd had to check his toes when she'd seen him swaying at the back glass door, because she'd barely recognized him, either. But he was my cat. *My cat.*

The vet literally couldn't find a heartbeat and told me I had a zombie cat. I didn't care, as long as the zombie was Digit. He purred and growled and leaned against me as hard as he could as he shook on the metal table.

The vet guessed he'd been walking since he disappeared. The pads on his feet and his claws were worn right off. He'd disappeared at the beginning of February; this was late June. Sometimes, the vet said, cats jumped in cars or truck beds to sleep in winter when they were cold and then ended up being transported far away. Walking at a cat's pace, he could have been as far away as Seattle. Leaving him at the vet's for treatment after he'd walked for four months to get to me was agony. I felt my own claws being pulled out as I heard him whine, too weak to howl as I left.

But he needed surgery for his demolished rear end, and that would only happen after they stabilized him, which would take days. If he made it. I couldn't bear to think about losing him again, and handed over my credit card, knowing it was close to maxed out. The cost didn't matter. We'd pay it somehow. He had to be fixed.

I went home and blogged Digit's return. I wrote about having had four or five dreams since he'd left that he'd shown up, alive, so very there, and how when I'd been kneeling in the kitchen, I'd asked Lala over and over if I was dreaming. "No," she'd said, stroking his head with a careful finger, "You're not."

Within hours of posting, hundreds of comments flooded in. A friend suggested I ask the knitters to raise money for his medical bills. I laughed. There were a million good causes to which people could give their hard-earned money. Digit was just a cat. (Just *the* cat, but that was beside the point.)

I couldn't ask for money. I didn't know how, and I didn't want to. But it gave me a thought: what if I held a drawing? Anyone who donated anything would get a chance to win sweaters, the very ones they'd watched me knit (and swear over) on the blog throughout the years. I included an alpaca V-neck pullover, soft gray with a purple Fair Isle design at the hem and cuffs that I was proud of—it had been my very first successful design. I also put up the first true Fair Isle sweater I'd ever made, a Philosopher's Wool kit (stranded colorwork, requiring one to carry different yarn in both hands at the same time). I included sweaters I loved. I didn't want it to be easy to part with them. It was only right.

I hoped perhaps I'd raise a hundred dollars. Maybe two. That would have thrilled me.

But the knitters pulled out their wallets and gave so much that my hands started to shake and didn't stop for two days. In amounts of mostly small denominations, five or ten dollars at a time, these knitters who read my blog and loved my cat raised more than seven thousand dollars. I blogged immediately that we'd raised more than enough for his treatment, but people kept giving. I pledged to give the overage to local animal-rescue organizations.

Knitters all over the world had come to the aid of a beat-up old cat, proving the cat/knitter stereotype both true and lovely. And I had to finally learn how to say, simply, thank you. How could I possibly say it so that people would know I meant it? How would they know that every single dollar, and every single thought, made a difference in my life, and therefore, in Digit's life? I tried to write it, tried to blog it, but nothing felt adequate to convey my feelings. Everything came down to those two simple words, and I learned that sometimes you just have to say them, and mean them, and hope that it's enough. It was okay that I didn't feel worthy of the money. I knew Digit was worthy, and that made it okay.

When we finally took him home, I resolved to never let him out again. He could howl all he wanted and pee where he might, but he wasn't going out. Never, ever again. But he didn't seem to want to go. He didn't cry (except for food) and he didn't use anything but the litter box to relieve himself.

I had my tonsils out not long afterward, and we recovered together, he with a cone on his head, still trying to knead and suck on my clothing, me with a puffed throat, unable to talk. I cast on for a sweater and knitted in bed, putting my gratitude into the stitches. I didn't eat bonbons, but I did eat a lot of Jell-O, and I read as many romance novels as I could get my hands on. Digit sat by my side and thumped any animal that got too close to me. Even with no claws and no strength, he packed a punch.

We slept as we always had, his many-toed paw in my hand, holding on to each other. My cat had found his way home, and I wasn't letting him go again. Growling in his sleep, claws latched lightly into my skin, he wasn't letting me go either.

STOCKINETTE

Growing up, I bossed both my sisters. All the time. About everything. I told Bethany she should use different colors when she was painting the mailbox. I told Christy that less glitter was sometimes more (I'll state for the record I was totally wrong about that). I told them to keep their greedy paws off my yarn stash, and God help them if I ever caught them using my long afghan-crochet hooks for swordplay—my wrath was fierce, my tattling tongue legendary, and when I cried to my parents, my halo couldn't have shined brighter or been more centrally perched above my head.

The fact is, both my sisters have always needed way less advice than I think they do. From how much eye shadow to wear in high school to what neighborhoods to consider renting apartments in, I've shared my opinions, even when they haven't wanted me to. Perhaps *especially* when they haven't wanted me to. I think it might be a big sister thing. God forbid someone push either of them around, though—there's only one person allowed to do that, and that's me.

For twenty years or more, I've nagged my middle sister Christy to learn the purl stitch. She stubbornly refuses to do so, enjoying the fruits of her rather infrequent knitting labors just fine with the one stitch she knows. "But look," I say. "This scarf has ribs, and it's only knit and purl. Doesn't it look fancy?"

She glances at it. "Pretty. Still don't want to."

In all honesty, she's naturally much more detail-oriented than I am. While I simply knitted as a kid (and often not well), she painted Ukrainian Easter eggs and built tiny dioramas inside walnut shells. When she decorated the walls of her bedroom with a snow scene, she didn't paint the details white on a blue background; instead, she painted the white wall blue around the intricate snowflakes. I, of course, thought she was half-baked for doing it that way, and told her so, up until it was done and gorgeous—then I took my friends on tours of her room to show off her cleverness.

And even now, she's the one with patience and forethought. Christy takes deliberate, well-thought-out steps toward a goal, just like she does when making art. When she achieves each goal, she can stand atop her accomplishment knowing she's made it there by choice, knowledge, and determination. While not the eldest, she was the first to leave our parents' house (I admit I clung to my mother's apron strings longer than most). Christy got her bachelor's degree from Mills College in Oakland, and then she went into environmental planning, getting paid to do what she was fascinated by. She applied to UC Berkeley, was accepted, and then graduated with a master's in city and regional planning. Goal, *check*. Next goal, *check*.

Me, on the other hand . . . my only real goals were to fall in love as much as possible, and to write. While I got pretty good at the love thing, I spent years not writing anything but journal entries. Sometimes I reached goals by just getting lucky. Sure, I might have made it over the divide, but I only leaped because I didn't know how wide the gulf was in the first place and how ridiculous I was to try. Query a national magazine and land an article with no previous national writing experience? Sure! An MFA in writing? Why not? Christy went to Mills College in order to obtain the tools to make our world a better place. I, on the other hand, only went to grad school because a boyfriend wanted me to get a master's sooner rather than the later I'd planned on, and I went to Mills College because I remembered how pretty the campus had been when I'd visited Christy there.

Christy brought that same focus and determination she'd applied to school and her career to her knitting. She learned how to knit in second grade from her teacher. Note that she did not learn from me, more evidence of her intelligence; when we fought as kids, we could be brutal, and knitting needles make gruesome weapons. She picked up knitting again in her twenties, creating perfect garter stitch in one rectangular form followed by another. She used gorgeous yarns and didn't drop stitches, and she ignored me every time I tried to nag her into learning how to purl. She'd been listening to me Know Better for many years by then. She didn't care if I thought her scarf should be longer, or wider, or narrower, or a different color. She'd learned long ago how to tune me out.

In spite of my faults, Christy gave me the very first scarf

she ever made. A fuzzy blue chenille scarf with long bits of fringe, it remains my favorite scarf not just because of its pillowy softness, but because she gave that first piece of knitting away.

When she handed me the wrapped package, her face was worried. "It's not very good," she said. "You might not like it." She closed her eyes and her face squinched up as I opened it. But the scarf was as lovely as her selfless act, and I adored it.

As Christy plotted strategic waypoints along her route, and I leaped before looking, our little sister Bethany bobbed through the waves of growing up a bit more gracefully. She's always been more of a dabbler, trying everything that crosses her path with fascinated interest. As a child, she picked up whatever craft was floating around at the time. She used my crochet hooks and Christy's tiny paintbrushes. During the lanyard craze, we had plastic rope key chains coming out of our ears. I remember her making hemp bracelets, friendship pins, felt banners, and macaroni trivets. And of course, I always had a great idea how she could do things better. She listened to me, and usually obligingly did as I said.

"When you color in your princess's fingernails, you should use the red crayon. Not that blue one. That's dumb."

"Oh." Her eyes widened as she reached for the red stub of wax. "Okay."

I was also often full of great ideas about how she should get me a glass of water if I was on the couch and how she should fetch my book for me if I'd left it in the other room. She'd sigh and protest weakly. I'd say it again, alternately cajoling or threatening if the bossing hadn't worked. Off she'd trudge to do my bidding. I loved being the big sister. Boy, had our parents gotten our birth order right, I thought.

After she turned sixteen, though, things abruptly changed. Bethany drove like I knitted—sometimes with a purpose, sometimes just to see what happened. She didn't often get lost, but when she did, she made great discoveries. As I worked out the best possible left-slanting double decrease, she figured out how to find the best back roads with the most curves.

And somehow, driving straightened her spine. One day —we both remember this quite vividly—I told her to grab me a Kleenex.

"No," she said.

"What? You're closer than I am. Just get me one."

"Get it yourself, lazyass." She says that she realized at that moment that she didn't have to do one damn thing I told her to. The fact that this realization occurred right around the same time she learned that turning the wheel could take her just about anywhere she wanted to go wasn't a coincidence.

But just because she stopped obeying my every whim didn't mean she didn't stop listening to me when I had *good* ideas. I encouraged her to indulge her dearest dream: to travel the United States before leaving them to explore other parts of the globe. Raised by parents who loved to wander, we'd all seen a good deal of the world but very little of our own country. Bethany had huge dreams of seeing every state, driving on the "blue highways," stopping wherever fancy struck her. Neil Gaiman's *American Gods* and its House on the Rock had affected her deeply, and she wanted to see for herself roadside attractions like huge pineapples and statues of Paul Bunyan and his blue ox. Christy and I worried she'd be murdered while sleeping in a Walmart parking lot in Nebraska, but the eighteen months she spent touring the country alone left her very much alive, not murdered even once.

During her travels, Bethany tried to figure out what she could give me for my birthday that would be both appreciated and, more importantly, cheap. She wanted something knitting related, but she was stumped as to what she could give me that I didn't already have in triplicate. I had enough row markers, and Bethany knew I certainly had enough yarn to tide me over till the apocalypse.

Then it hit her. The scarf from Christy had been so well received—what if she made me a *sweater*?

She'd been knitting hats and scarves, so she wasn't a total newbie. Choosing a simple pullover pattern, she knitted for months, keeping it a secret. If she'd been in the Bay Area, she wouldn't have been able to hide it from me. She would have slipped, unable to resist asking me a knitting question. Instead, far away, she had to choose her own method of casting on, and when the pattern said to put the sleeves on holders, she had to trust she was guessing how to do it correctly.

In town for a short while before getting back on the road, she gave me my birthday gift. Just as Christy had, she looked worried as she pushed the present toward me.

"I'm not really sure about this," she said.

I pulled out the beautifully heathered gray wool sweater and immediately words abandoned me. Eventually I was able to stutter something inane like, "You made me a sweater?"

Her face fell. "You don't like it?"

I didn't know how to say it. It was wonderful. The sweater fit me perfectly, better than anything I'd ever made myself. It had waist shaping that curved inward where I did, and the V-neck was just the right depth. It was cozy. And no one ever knits for a knitter. I felt loved when I put it on, just as I did when I wrapped Christy's scarf around my neck. Safe. If this was what everyone felt when they put on hand-knits, then I wondered how people who didn't have any got along in the world. On cold, foggy Bay Area mornings, I'd be able to wear my scarf and my sweater and remember that my sisters loved me for who I was, bossy boots and all, and I'd remind myself that we weren't children anymore—my little sisters had grown up, and so had I.

Bethany would end up touring forty-seven states, sleeping in the truck's rear camper shell. She picked up odd jobs when she ran out of money and took showers at truck stops. She knitted mittens and hats through a cold winter in Minneapolis, where she worked nights at a hostel, and spent the next winter in a cabin in Montana, knitting herself a pink cabled cardigan while she retiled a bathroom floor.

After she came home briefly to give me my present and spend a weekend camping with the family, she took off again to complete her trip. Christy and I saw her off from an Old West–style bar in a tiny mining town named Copperopolis. We both bossed her senseless as we ate our fries. *Lock your doors! Call if you need money! Don't take any wooden nickels! People named Shiv should never be trusted! Don't forget to floss!*

She drove north, ignoring all the little reminders we tossed at her, cheerfully waving her hand out the window as we swiped at our wet faces. I told Christy sharply to stop crying, and she told me to shut it, and then we clung to each other in the dusty parking lot, watching Bethany's red pickup disappear in the distance.

Ten Years Later

I had dinner last night with my sisters, who are my best friends. We ate ahi tuna and baklava and laughed until we cried. Then we cried until we laughed. This is not hyperbole. I'm scared to death of leaving them. The scarf Christy made and the sweater Bethany made are in the hope chest along with my wedding shawl. The chest will soon be on a cargo ship, bobbing over the ocean toward New Zealand, and Lala and I will be on a plane headed away from my sisters. Lala plans to spend the fourteen-hour flight watching all of the Lord of the Rings movies. I plan on spending them crying, drying my tears just in time to step off the plane into my new country. Without asking, I know both of my sisters want me to move forward from a place of courage, not fear. Their bravery is inside me, and because of that, I will be able to leave them.

Just barely.

MAIDENS AND FLYERS

I've had plenty of obsessions over the years, from macramé to rock climbing. New skills take over my brain at regular intervals, leaving me little room or desire to think of anything else. But the urge to spin wool blindsided me with its intensity and connected me to a past I'd never considered.

For years, I'd refused to spin, saying I wasn't interested. I didn't want to try to understand how those pretty wheels worked. They looked so intricate with their dark wood and carved gears. The sound of the treadle seduced me with its rhythmic thump. But I didn't have another free minute, and spinning was just another time suck. I was busy enough with a full-time job, writing, and knitting.

Then I touched a wheel, unable to resist my friends' encouragement any longer. Like Sleeping Beauty, I fell into a trance, except my eyes stayed open—and the fiber flew.

Of course, it was nothing but carnage when first I sat down to try spinning at my friend Janine's wheel. The fiber kept spinning into great, undraftable clumps, or drifting into fine whispers of twist, floating apart in my hands. The more I tried to grab it, the more it slipped away from me. I barely resisted the urge to stomp my feet and throw a tantrum. A fiber craft! One that I couldn't learn instantly! Oh, I was *steamed*.

Again and again, I snared the leader with the hook, drew it out, and tried my very best to hold the fiber as my friend Janine had said, like it was a baby bird, though I was pretty sure an actual fledgling would have needed some birdie CPR by that point.

With Janine's encouragement, I kept turning the wheel. My feet moved. I drew my arm back. Then, suddenly, something fell into place. I looked at my left hand and saw an amazing sight: loose fiber turning into yarn. Finally, I held the fiber loosely enough. I'm surprised I didn't hear the *bing* as the light bulb went on over my head, but Janine saw it happen, and she pointed it out: that point, just past my fingertips by a few millimeters, that was where the magic was. It didn't happen at the wheel, or where the yarn entered the orifice to wind around the bobbin. The wheel itself, a thing that looks like it should do all the work, doesn't. Your hand does the work, as it draws back and plays against the tension the wheel provides while it inserts twist into those loose fibers.

In a way, it felt better than knitting. In knitting I created a concrete *something*. In spinning, I was creating a *pre*something. Yarn, not yet knitted, held an almost infinite number of possibilities.

Oh, I was born to spin.

I wasn't some wunderkind spinner—my yarns were lumpy and, well . . . homespun looking. But within an hour of learning, I was making decent yarn and, within a day, I was beyond hooked. I loved the speed with which the finished product came from my fingers and whirled around the bobbin. In a short amount of time, I could go from owning a pile of fluff to owning gorgeous one-of-a-kind yarn.

I needed my own wheel. I *had* to have one of my own. But the next fiber festival was all the way across the country: Maryland Sheep and Wool. I understood it was ridiculous to fly that far when I could just do some research and probably find a wheel I liked locally. But a festival would display *all* of the different makes and models. I'd get to try whichever one struck my fancy. I'd have choice.

Travel so far to feed a new obsession? Who would do that?

My breathing shallow, I closed my eyes and clicked the Buy button for the airplane ticket.

Once at the festival, I scooped up armful after armful of unspun fiber. Nothing was safe from me: Rambouillet, Corriedale, Targhee, Cormo, I wanted it all, and I wanted it in every color of the rainbow. How could I guess what my first handspun sweater should be made from if I hadn't tried spinning it? I bought sweater quantities of everything, just to be safe.

And then I found the wheel of my heart, an Ashford Joy. I bought it on the spot. I was blowing through money like it was water, but I felt such a need to spin that it was almost a physical urge, like hunger or sleep. I didn't understand where the need came from; I just fed it.

In order to fly home with my bounty, I put the fiber into a large plastic tub from Target and sealed it with duct tape. I thought it was a great idea. I'd just check the behe-moth, and my loot would meet me on the baggage carousel at the other end.

Then the airline representative said, baggage sticker in his hand, "Can you open that for me, please?"

"What?" I asked in horror. I couldn't open it. There was no way. I'd used the whole roll of tape. I'd had to sit on it to get it closed.

"I just need to do a visual check, since I can't see what's in it."

I didn't think before speaking, and the words tumbled from my mouth. "I can't open it. It'll *explode*!"

Everything in the terminal stopped and went into slow motion. Heads turned, mouths agape. I heard a high-pitched whine in my ears. The representative took a slow and deliberate step backward.

"We have a problem," he said.

I leaped forward, further terrifying the poor man, and launched into DEFCON 1 Wild Spinner speak: "You can't open it, I didn't mean to say that. It's just fiber! You know, pre-yarn? I'm going to spin it all when I get home. I have this dream of making my own handspun sweater, from scratch, like some I saw this weekend, and some is dyed already but some is natural, and maybe I'll dye it. I haven't decided. But if we open it, it will never, ever, *ever* close again, and who's going to help me get all that fiber back in there? You? No, I don't think so." I put my head down on the counter and wailed, "I don't have any more *tape*."

I must have been the man's first banana-pants spinner because I confused him so much that he just let me through. Hurriedly, he slapped the baggage label on the bin and gave me my boarding pass, shaking his head the whole time.

I wasn't done with the Baltimore airport, though. I didn't check my new beloved Ashford Joy; instead, I carried it on in its clever backpack. As it passed through the X-ray machine, the person running the scanner paled. He glanced up at me and then back at the screen.

"I, um, need to send that back through again."

"Okay," I said.

He let out a long, low whistle and then said, "Hey, Steve, you gotta get a look at this." It took a little talking to get it through, but by now I was becoming adept at Inane Spinner Speak. They let me pass, confusion still in their eyes.

In the terminal, waiting to board our plane, I couldn't wait. I took my new beauty from its case and attached a leader. I unpacked the bit of fiber (purple merino and silk) that I'd put in the front pocket of the bag, just in case. I gave it a good oiling.

People started to stare.

I didn't care. I began to spin.

I got a few comments from passersby, most of them along the lines of "Whoa." One woman snapped, "I can't believe they let you in here with that. Shouldn't be allowed."

I ignored the comment, but it made me nervous, and I noticed a turbaned security officer had picked me up on his radar. I watched him pace back and forth, frowning at me. He got closer and closer. Was he mentally reviewing his handbook? Where was the Giant Wooden Spinning Thing section? Could it be a weapon?

Did he have a responsibility to do something about this?

Finally, he approached. I didn't stop spinning, but my heart beat faster, and I lost control of the fiber. It drifted to bits, and I had to look down at the wheel, using the orifice hook to pull the yarn back out again. The woman who had snapped at me watched with anticipation.

"You're spinning," he said in an Indian accent. He still scowled.

"Yes," I said. If he took it from me, would I get it back? Or would they destroy it? I couldn't let that happen. If I picked it up by its handle and sprinted for the gate, would he give chase? He looked like he'd move slowly, and, after all, I'd already threatened airport security with an explosion and gotten away with it, what was one more security infraction?

"I used to spin," he said, the scowl giving way to something softer. "It's what my people did. At home. I used a charka. Do you know what that is?"

I nodded, so surprised I could barely speak. "It's for cotton, right?"

He smiled and sighed, bending his knees to come into a low squat next to the wheel. We were eye to eye. "Yes, cotton. It's lovely. Peaceful. I wish I could do it now, but I don't have one. Why do you spin?"

I wasn't sure how to answer. "Because I have to. I'm not sure why."

"It's what your people did?"

My eyes widened as I realized for the first time, yes, he was right. It was what my people did. My father grew up riding his uncle's horses on the ranch, herding sheep and cattle. My mother was raised in New Zealand, the daughter of a sheep farmer. One of my first clear memories is of being in a New Zealand shearing barn, sliding down the wool chute, and landing in piles of freshly shorn fiber. I own a handspun wool blanket that was woven by my great-grandmother.

I come from wool people, from spinners and knitters. They are my heritage, and I was claiming it. I realized that's why the hunger felt so natural, why the urge was so keen.

The grin could have split my face in two. My new friend and I talked spinning until they called my flight. The offended woman who had snapped at me stopped staring and pouted into a book.

I should have known that, for me, spinning was inevitable.

It's what my people did.

Ten Years Later
That wheel has seen some serious miles. It's now wobbly and clunky and desperately needs a tune-up. For a little while, I considered not taking it with us to New Zealand. I could get a new one there, right?

But I couldn't quite bear to leave it behind. Along with the cedar chest, it's the only thing I'm bringing that's not packed in a box. Lala's bringing eight or nine of her guitars and banjos (she's sold *so* many more than that). My wheel is my instrument, quite literally. When we go camping at music festivals, people stay up jamming until the wee hours. I always have my ukulele nearby, but usually, I just spin while others play. I'm not good at playing an instrument and singing at the same time, but when I spin, my voice travels up into the trees, winding around other voices in harmony as my feet work the treadle. It's not only what my people did, now it's what *I* do. I can't wait to get my New Zealand Ashford Joy a tune-up in her own country. I'm bringing her home.

CHAIN STITCH

*I*t's hard to remember how we built our yarn stashes before the internet came along. I don't mean just that we all started buying yarn online when it became possible to do so (although we did—I remember that fateful day I typed "yarn" into brand-new eBay's search field and then *freaked out*), I just mean that the world, as a whole, got so much bigger, didn't it?

Pre-internet, I shopped for yarn at chain craft stores. Michael's, JoAnn's, Beverly's: I hit all the stores with a person's first name. I knew in the back of my mind that "real" yarn stores existed, but I didn't know then what that meant. Even though I lived in the Bay Area, I'd never gone to one. I thought they would just charge me too much and I was happy with my wool/acrylic combos.

Then the internet happened. I say that as if I woke up one morning and the whole World Wide Web was just there, which isn't true at all. I remember watching it grow over time, but, looking back, it feels like it just popped up one night. And on the internet, thanks to the knitting blogs

I started reading, I discovered that people sought out and bought specific kinds of yarn.

It was a revelation that people out there were knitting with yarn that I didn't even know about, that I immediately wanted to have. Of course, that wouldn't do. So I started buying yarn online, and boy, it was so easy! Just a few clicks, enter a few numbers, and bam! My very own postal carrier would bring lovely, light boxes full of color right to my door. It was miraculous.

I disappeared right down the rabbit hole for a while. For years, in fact. I shopped for yarn all over the world except in my own backyard, where it just didn't occur to me to look (I'm crafty, but not always that swift). And along with being able to order yarn online, I was suddenly able to research yarn before I traveled, and I discovered a passion: yarn travel.

I was finally able to locate yarn stores *before* I hit the road. Instead of hoping I'd run into yarn, I'd go directly to the yarn shop that I'd already researched. And I'd wager that all knitters, even on the strictest of yarn diets, invoke the Souvenir Yarn Clause when we travel. Souvenir yarn—especially if it's just sock yarn—doesn't count. We can buy as much as we want of it, because obviously, it's just a tiny bit of yarn. It hardly costs anything when compared to the trip itself, and sock yarn will always fit in your carry-on for the ride home.

With the Souvenir Yarn Clause held firmly in mind, I went to the New York Sheep and Wool Festival in Rhinebeck, New York, and the orange lace-weight cashmere I found there justified the whole trip. In Lake Tahoe, I found Cormo batts. In Atlanta I discovered Miss Babs's hand-painted yarns, and I also found the best key lime pie I've ever had, so that was kind of a double win. I bought blue merino in Belgium after spending two hours walking across the city. I purchased possum wool in New Zealand and learned that cats think this is the most interesting yarn of all. I've gotten hand-dyed lace-weight in British Columbia and good sturdy cream wool just outside London. Venice has provided so much yarn throughout the years that I'm actually a little embarrassed to think about it.

And the best part? In most of those towns I met other knitters, friends that I'd already made online and finally got to hug in person. There weren't as many of us blogging back then, and you could go around the entire knit-blog circle in an hour or two of web surfing. I'd never before knitted with anyone, had never dreamed of something as exotic as knitting out together in public. Sheesh, at-home knitting wasn't even something you copped to. You did it in private. This getting together to knit was a whole new world.

And now I had friends in faraway cities who *got* me. They knew how I felt when I sat on my favorite bamboo needles (hint: not good), and they understood why I couldn't resist collecting yarn on my travels the way other people collect snow globes or shot glasses. When I'd come to town on a trip, we'd sit around tables knitting, and no matter what city in the world I was in, the conversation always went the same way: from yarn to needles to patterns and, finally, to knit-blog gossip, the most delicious kind of all.

Those were the good old days, though. The economic

lean times hit our home just like it did many others. Bills needed to be paid more than trips needed to be taken. I tried to take it in stride, but I was still depressed about it. Yarn traveling was something I loved doing, and I wouldn't be able to do it much anymore. I tried not to think about it and stopped buying yarn, knitting out of my stash. Thank goodness I'd stocked up.

Finally, I opened my eyes and looked around. It should have been obvious, of course, but somehow, seeing what was practically in my backyard, hiding in plain sight, was astonishing. My immediate neighborhood, I found, was chock-full of the yarn and knitters that I'd been traveling so far to find.

My local yarn shop is Article Pract (a spoonerism of "practical art"). There, I'll find the owner, Christina Stork, who is way cooler than I'll ever be. She wears awesome clothes I could never get away with and has naturally red hair and a smile that reaches from one ear to the other. Her boyfriend coaches roller derby, and she knits while she screams encouragement from ringside. Tattooed and pierced indie artists staff the counter, and I'm always kind of thrilled when someone knows me there, as if I'm walking in to the Cheers of yarn (except they're calling Rachael! instead of Norm!). It gives me a little boost I can't quite get from buying Malabrigo online. (Oh, the softness of that stuff! It makes up for the vinegar smell left over from its dyeing process.) It doesn't hurt that Christina's store is in the district that is currently the hippest in Oakland, and it's surrounded by restaurants that all seem to have been started by ex-employees of Chez Panisse. In the same vein, Christina is the Alice Waters of yarn, putting everyone in contact with everyone else, our yarn-locavore, making sure we are able to stay local.

But Christina is more than a yarn vendor to me. She's more than just stash-acquisition. Now that she's moved to live practically within shouting distance of my house, I've been over to see her ducks, to sit in her kitchen and eat salad drizzled with raspberry vinaigrette and warm, locally made bread. We don't even knit much when we're together; we're usually too busy catching up, our hands flapping in time with our words, not noticing we haven't knitted until the end of our visit, when one brings out something to show the other. From Christina I learned that homemade soup, made at the end of a long workday, served to friends, is as nourishing to the soul as it is to the body. She taught me that there's never time in the week to see friends—no one has any free hours anymore—but you do it anyway, and you don't regret staying up a little past your bedtime in order to catch up with someone you love. You can't learn that on the internet.

Another thing you can't do on the internet is sit around knitting on a random Saturday afternoon while appreciating vegan food. Yes, I eat meat, and I won't try to convince you to do otherwise. But my knitting friends Kira and Rachel Dulaney are generous and hospitable, and they're known for hosting crafting parties that feature everything from Indian bhindi masala to homemade sushi, always vegan and always delicious.

Having known them for a long time now, I can look at my relationship with them to define how my relationship with yarn has changed throughout the years. Rachel lived with my little sister Bethany in the dorms at San Francisco

State. We hung out but we didn't talk knitting, because I didn't talk knitting with anyone. I just did it at home, privately.

Then the internet opened knitting up—I believe that the reason knitting became trendy was because knitting information became so readily disseminated and available online. People started to talk about it. One afternoon, Kira, whom I'd known for a year or two by then, was wearing a pair of fingerless gloves.

"Those are pretty," I said, admiring the cables on the back.

"I made them," Kira said.

When I pulled myself out of the vegan sushi platter that I'd fallen into, we talked yarn nonstop for the next hour while Rachel sat patiently listening. Since then, Kira's moved on from being a talented knitter to managing a yarn store to owning her own design business, KiraK Designs. She's been featured in national knitting magazines and is well known in the industry now. But I still think of her as our adorable know-it-all who drops everything to deliver groceries if someone needs them. Both she and Rachel give their time and energy to anyone who needs anything, driving friends to doctors' appointments, dropping off spare cable needles when needed. They both came to my mother's funeral and, afterward, sang songs from the musical *Chess* at the top of their lungs in the kitchen with us. If I were ever put in jail and my family refused to take my calls, they'd be the ones I'd phone next.

Don't get me wrong, traveling the world to buy yarn, meeting knit-friends along the way, is fantastic. If you can afford the money and time, you should try it. You can take a knitting cruise to Alaska, or a knit-themed tour of Northern Italy, and you can spend many, many hours happily researching all of it before you go. It's wonderful to buy fiber in a language you don't speak with currency you barely understand. The language of yarn is always the same, and a Swedish knitter can show an Aussie how to cast on without using words.

But having yarn sources and yarn people in your own town is better. Having someone you can call on to show you in person exactly how to do that wild Cat Bordhi Moebius cast-on, the one that makes you double a long needle and knit around and around, top and bottom, increasing from inside out, making your brain explode in the process, is priceless. That just wasn't something I could learn online from YouTube videos, although I tried—I had to tap Morgaine of San Francisco's Carolina Homespun (which I knew because of the internet) and beg her to show me. Morgaine was my friend. She was local. Of course she showed me.

And what are yarn friends for, after all?

Ten Years Later
  I thought I knew about knitterly love back then, but I really had no idea. A young woman named Tawnie emailed me after reading this book, telling me about her beloved cat. It was the start of one of the most important relationships of my life. I call Tawnie my goddaughter now, because it's a word that people under-stand. It's the closest word I can come up with for what she is to me. We were brought into each other's lives for a

reason, and she's one of the brightest spots in my life. I'm never more happy than I am when we're on the same couch, knitting and watching terrible and awesome reality TV. The joy that runs through my bones is almost terrifying in its immensity.

One night, I was at the launch party for my thriller *Stolen Things.* In a bookstore in San Francisco, the room was standing room only, full of the people I love best. I was in conversation with a best friend, Sophie Littlefield, both of us talking about the craft of writing. An audience member asked us, "Do you think a lot about theme when you're writing?"

Obviously, this question came from a writer, and I loved it. "I do. I think that we all have core themes, the themes lodged deeply in our hearts, and they come up again and again in all the work we do. I can't get away from two themes. Even if I try to write something else, the story always ends up coming back to the mother-daughter relationship and chosen family."

In the back of the room, I spotted Tawnie smiling at me. She'd been with me all day as we buzzed around getting things ready for the reading. My heart doubled, then tripled in size—I was so glad she'd been able to come up from San Diego to be there on that day.

Then it hit me. "Oh, wow," I said. "My goddaughter is here, and I just realized that with her, I have both those things. The mother-daughter relationship *and* chosen family."

Next to me, my friend Sophie beamed. She already knew that, obviously. And even though Tawnie was at the back of the room, I could see her get teary. I swallowed around the lump of happiness lodged in my throat. "I'm so *lucky.*"

It *is* immense luck that we found each other. Tawnie and I share the same rare, incurable, life-threatening disease that almost no one else has, hereditary angioedema type III, a confusing disease that sometimes takes dozens of years to diagnose. I recognized the symptoms in her, so she was diagnosed earlier than most, perhaps saving her life.

But it's more than luck—it's this *book*, the one that in a very meta way is about moms and daughters and chosen families. I wrote it. She read it. She emailed me. We began a lifelong relationship that nothing will ever be able to sever. She's my heart.

Thanks, knitting.

NEGATIVE EASE

The first time I went to Europe, I was twenty-four years old. My sister Christy was studying abroad, and we traveled together through as many countries as we could cram into her spring break. I carried yarn in my backpack (it came in handy for shoelaces and clotheslines several times) and we stayed in hostels, littering *Rick Steves* pages behind us as we went. Traveling through Italy, we only stopped in Venice because Christy wanted to. I'd thought Venice would be like Disneyland, all glitz and painted sets featuring overpriced boat rides.

We approached the city on the train at night, riding across the long span, the ugly steam stacks of Mestre puffing behind us, the twinkling lights ahead of us. I knitted as the city floated closer, not expecting much.

Then we exited the train station and saw the Scalzi Bridge spanning the Grand Canal, a deep velvet sky hanging heavily above. My heart tipped drunkenly inside my chest, as I tripped and fell into love. My heavy backpack suddenly weighed nothing. I could have walked all night—and we almost did, trying to find our elusive hotel room in the dark, winding streets.

I've been back as many times as possible, and Venice is the city of my heart. It's beautiful, of course, but also tricky. *La Serenissima* keeps her secrets from most of those who tromp through on a one-day pass, those tourists who never get off the crowded main *calles* and complain about the canal's fragrance on warm days. But if you wait, if you're patient and very lucky, Venice will reveal both her schemes and her charms in her own good time.

In Venice, the light is refracted up into the salty air in a million splintered pieces, and the sounds of the city—boat engines humming on the canal, heels clacking on the cobblestones, men singing outside *osterie*—make me feel like I'm finally home. Once I was lucky enough to rent an apartment just around the way from the casino, and I pretended I lived there, making my coffee in the *caffettiera*, drinking it on my terrace overlooking the red roofs. While I ate the crusty bread and thinly sliced sharp cheese I'd bought at the local grocery store, I listened to the bells chime around the ancient city. Never in sync with each other, they made my head swim with their richness.

I was thrilled when I got to go there with my wife. Lala's band was touring in Belgium, and I thought as long as she was getting paid to go to Europe, I should show her my favorite city. Once there, I took her to the most spectacular secret views and to the most delicious gelato place in town. I showed her the Snail Staircase and the jewel-like hidden bathroom in San Marco.

"You know your way everywhere," she said. "How do you not get lost?"

"I don't know. I just don't."

"Don't lose me. There's no way I'd ever find the hotel again."

"Stick with me, kid." I turned down a tiny *calle* and led her into the best music shop in town.

Of course, I didn't skip shopping for yarn. There isn't much of it in Venice, but it's there if you know where to look. As you pass the lingerie shops that face the main streets, look farther inside, past the hanging bustiers and garter belts, and there, on the back wall, you can sometimes find a few rows of Italian yarn, hidden in plain sight. And then there's LellaBella, which sits just on the far right-hand side of a tiny bridge as you walk toward San Marco from the Rialto. No knitter worth her double points can miss it, and it's well worth a stop—it only carries Italian yarn, and while it's not inexpensive, the owner of the shop and her mother are helpful and friendly. That day, I found six skeins of merino yarn, a variegated soft pink and lavender. I'm usually drawn to rich ochre, red, or yellow, the colors of the city's roofs, so I don't know why I picked it off the shelf and bought it—I just knew I needed it.

And when I got home to Oakland, I don't know why I was drawn to cast on for a sweater in a pattern I'd already made (Debbie Bliss's "Lara"). Knitted sideways, it was a puzzle of a sweater, and I loved the surprise of it: Just fold and sew a seam and presto! You get a sweater! It was a magic trick worthy of Elizabeth Zimmerman. But with so many patterns in the world, I didn't need two of any sweater. So I wasn't sure how I knew that *this* was the right pattern. But I knew.

Right away, I wasn't sure about the size I'd chosen. It

didn't seem quite long enough or wide enough, but it was hard to tell while knitting a sweater that wouldn't be recognizable until that last seam. And even when I was a week or two into the knitting, I still wasn't sure about the color. Pink! What was I thinking?

I kept going, though. When I finished, it didn't fit. *Of course* it didn't fit. I'd seen it coming—why was I surprised?

I felt that Venice had let me down a little—the first time the city had ever done so—and I was disappointed. Usually when I brought things home from Venice, even when I didn't know what they were meant to be, they revealed their true purpose when I got home. The ashtray I bought after I quit smoking became the jewelry tray in the bathroom. The glass snail I bought in Murano weighted down the stamps on my desk. The paperback I picked up on a whim in the English bookstore was the first in a series of mysteries my mother and I would love for years. Maybe I'd thought that the pink sweater would magically become my favorite, that I'd be suddenly slim enough to fit into it when it was done. Or that I'd put it on and my ruddy complexion would instantaneously become delicately colored, all peaches and cream. I blogged about my failure, briefly showing the sweater in repose on a chair and then put it on my stack of completed knits. I immediately cast on for a different sweater, just glad to be done with the pink merino.

Weeks later, I got an email from a woman named Joan. In a short note, she wrote that she'd recently lost her husband after a motorcycle accident before she got to take him to Venice, her favorite city. She'd thought about offering to take the Venetian sweater off my hands, but that would be "the ultimate in cheek" from someone I didn't even know.

It wasn't cheek. I felt it as soon as I read the email, and I wrote back, asking for her address. I told her that when I was knitting it, I knew it was wrong—the colors, the size— but I'd had to keep knitting it, and now I knew why.

Venice had known she needed it, and I'd been making it for her.

I sent the sweater, and she mailed back a letter that made me cry.

Him? The bluest eyes I'd ever seen, a moustache, a tattoo, and a 750cc Norton Commando motorcycle . . . Over the years, the only thing that changed was the number of motorcycles: when he died, I was left with five to deal with.

What happened? In early June 2006, my darling man, who started riding in 1968 or '69 and had thousands and thousands of miles under his wheels, was coming home on a solo ride to a vintage bike gathering in NorCal and was knocked off by a kid making an un-signaled, illegal left turn into an unmarked track. The impact compound-fractured his tib/fib and the ER doc in Susanville told me that Gerry was likely to lose his leg, that he was being medivaced to Reno, and that he thought I should get down there. . . . Two days later, while waiting in the pre-op area for a routine clean and debride, he had a massive MI, was revived but never came back. He took three weeks to die.

Ger's blood volume was completely transfused. Twice. From total stranieri, *the gift of more time—time to get our heads around what was happening, time for our daughter to come home from France, time for our son to go from kid to adult, time to realize that his side of the bed was going to stay empty.*

I was so happy I had something to give her. And then

our lives went on, and she left comments on the blog from time to time, and sometimes I'd wonder if the sweater had any use, or if it had ended up in the back of her closet. Either case was fine—it was her sweater. It always had been. But years later, curiosity got the best of me, and I emailed her: "What happened with the sweater? Did you end up wearing it?"

Her answer was incredible. She sent the missive via email but she'd asked that I imagine it was written in fountain pen (wide-nibbed), black ink on yellow-lined eight-and-a-half-by-eleven paper, and I did.

Rachael, I wear your sweater at least twice a week through the winter and well into the spring. I wore it so often that first year that one of my students asked if I only had one sweater. I think of La Serenissima *and her colors floating on my shoulders, and I remember that I will go back and that I will take some of Ger's ashes to share with her waters. I will never dance with him in San Marco, never ride a* traghetto *with him, never take my glass-worker to Murano, never wait patiently while he takes another picture of canal repairs. I wrap myself in your sweater, though, and know that all that is good of him and me is still here and you are part of that learning and I am so grateful for you. I consider you and Lala friends not yet met. I hope you don't mind.*

I realized that Venice had given both of us a gift we'd never imagined receiving. I'd bought the yarn, I'd knitted it, and I'd mailed the sweater away. I'd gone through my days afterward handling my own life and work, grief and joy, and seldom gave a thought to the sweater I'd sent northward (although I did think of Joan on warm summer evenings when motorcycles roared through Oakland—

she'd told me she still turned to look when they passed, just to see if Gerry was riding one of them).

The day she sent that letter was a rough day in our house. Lala and I had been arguing about stupid things, and I was fractious and annoyed. I had the thought that sometimes floats through a person's mind, "So this is why they say marriage is hard."

Then I read Joan's letter and remembered something.

When Lala and I were in Venice, we'd had a tremendous argument near the Doge's Palace after a dinner featuring too much wine. We rarely fight, but this one was a doozy and involved both of us stalking away from each other in fury when the words got too heated. Almost instantly I realized several things: Lala didn't know the name of the hotel where we were staying—I'd meant to put a business card from the front desk into her pocket, just in case, but I'd forgotten to do it. Neither of us had cell phones. And Lala had zero sense of direction in the confusing city and couldn't have even guessed which way to go.

I panicked. I looked back the way she'd walked, and I saw her going over a bridge on the Riva degli Schiavoni, near the Danieli. I ran as fast as I could through the midnight crowd, grabbing her shoulder when I caught up to her. "Oh, God, I thought that—"

It wasn't her. The woman gaped at me in surprise and then kept walking. I looked back over the two bridges I'd just raced across and couldn't see anyone who looked like her. I ran back, toward where I'd last seen her, calling her name. If I could only find her again, I'd apologize. I'd say all the things I hadn't said in our argument. I started to cry, and I'm sure I wasn't the first woman ever to wander past the gondolas with tears streaming down her cheeks.

Finally, I called her name again and heard, "I'm here."

Lala stepped forward. She'd been leaning on a lamppost next to the Bridge of Sighs, over which Casanova legendarily passed on his way into prison in the mid-eighteenth century.

"I thought I'd lost you."

She shook her head and took my hand. "Impossible."

We made up in St. Mark's Square, dancing in the moonlight to the dueling orchestras while rose vendors hawked their wares and eyed us suspiciously. She learned the name of our hotel by heart, and we drank less wine the following night.

But I remember that sense of desperation I felt during such a minor mishap. If I couldn't find her, with no way *to* find her, all in front of me turned to blackness, and there was no place for the light to creep in.

When Joan lost Gerry, she couldn't find him again. She had to stay behind while he left, and in no way does this seem fair or right or good or anything but too terrible to contemplate. But when she let herself write to a stranger about Venice, the city of her heart, *La Serenissima* had a gift waiting for her in Oakland.

Joan said, *You bought yarn and knit it into something that you knew wasn't working for you and yet you kept on going— something that is such an act of faith that "it will be all right in the end and if it's not all right, then it's not the end" and I have hung onto that fairly often.*

But it's her life, not my knitting, that is truly the act of faith. She keeps moving, keeps knitting, keeps living, day after day, stitch after stitch. I hate that Joan will never take Gerry to Venice. And her story reminds me of this: the fact that I still have my person is just pure dumb luck. For Joan's sake, I will not take that for granted.

For Joan's sake, when I'm short-tempered and tired, when I'm tempted to lash out, I will try to remember that frustration is fleeting and that love is what matters most. Lala, who lost her first wife to cancer, knows this. Joan knows this. And I vow I will try not to take a single day of togetherness for granted. It's not always easy, and I know I'll fall back into snapping at Lala about her music being too loud while I'm trying to sleep, and she'll complain that I *don't* listen to her. I'll protest loudly, knowing in my heart that sometimes she's right, I don't listen. But for Joan's sake, I'll try my damndest to hear more, to notice every single precious second given to us.

And this is my wish: I hope that in every roar of every motorcycle, Joan continues to hear Gerry's voice. I hope that when she stands at the Bridge of Sighs, she feels his lips at her temple, a brush of wind that feels familiar and necessary. And when the wind takes his ashes, I pray she finds peace. And I thank her, with all my heart, for the gift she's given me.

Ten Years Later
Since writing this, I've been back to the city of my heart five or six times. I'll think I'll stay away from Venice for a while, tired of her crowds and noise, and then, after about a year, I'll start to have recurring dreams in

which I'm trying to get into the city but can't quite find my way there. So I always go back.

I've been to Venice with all of the most important women in my life: both of my sisters on different trips, Lala, Tawnie, and my mother. After Mom died, I sneaked some ashes into the country with me, hoping customs wouldn't ask about the small baggie of powder. One night, I sat on the edge of a canal next to the Arsenale. My apartment was located in a very quiet section of town. There were no tourists around, and even the locals were all inside eating dinner. In the night's blue dimness, I raised my glass of wine to my mother, and then tipped the tiny bag into the canal. She loved the city as much as I did. Immediately, around the corner, I heard my mother's distinctive whistle. It was the way she called us in at night, and I've never heard anyone else do it.

In that moment, I knew we were together.

JOIN IN THE ROUND

I'm an early adopter. I love technology. If it's a new gadget, I embrace it and everything it comes with. I was banking online as soon the banks had websites. I had a blog before most people knew the word was short for web log. I bought a first-generation Kindle before I knew if I would like reading books digitally (which I do), and even though I told myself that I'd never buy an iPad, I owned one within a week of their release. I love the world we're living in. I adore that I have a *computer* in my *pocket*. With my cell phone, I can locate friends, look up menus, and give people directions to places I've never been. When I'm trying to decide whether to knit a particular pattern, I don't have to guess how the sleeves look if the pattern picture isn't enough—I look it up on Ravelry, the capital of our virtual knitting community, and consider how women shaped like me look in the sweater in question. We are living in the future, and it seems as if many knitters know it. While embracing the old craft of knitting, we're now making notes about our needle sizes on our iPhones, never thinking about how impossibly amazing this is.

I mean, sometimes I trip out just driving my car. *Oh, heavens . . . what a commute—how weary I am of sitting in a comfortable seat and pushing a pedal with the muscles of my big toe.* Even as a kid, I'd look out the car windows and pretend that Laura Ingalls Wilder had just teleported through time to sit next to me—what would she do? Scream? Faint? I'd point out the wonders of traveling at sixty miles per hour in a closed environment, and she'd be my best friend forever. Our world would fry her mind.

But even the simplest technology comes with a price tag that I haven't always been able to afford, and when I was in grad school, I didn't have even so much as a pager. The most technologically advanced thing I owned was my secondhand computer the size of a VW bug. With its dial-up modem, it took fifteen minutes to boot up, and God forbid the wind change when I was saving a document. More than one paper was lost to the blue screen of death and the sound of my wails echoing off the Oakland hills.

As I've mentioned before, I learned what cold meant during grad school. Cold and dry is not the same as cold and wet. Clammy lends a deeper, more bone-chilling cold-ness to a night, and a tiny apartment built into a damp hill-side in Oakland never dries out and never warms up. For someone who thought she didn't got cold, I learned quickly that I was just plain good old-fashioned wrong.

I saved up and bought an electric blanket. I loved it. It was the high-tech solution to my chilly problem, and I loved flipping on the switch and setting the dial to ten. This was good for a while, until my dad started calling me, telling me about the dangers of electromagnetic radiation. I disregarded his concern for the electromagnetic waves that would irradiate my body as I slept, until one night wiring in the walls shorted and I woke to an all-over body shock. My cat, Digit, who slept with me, screamed in pain, and I rocketed out of the bed as every plugged-in appliance in my apartment roared on—the lights, the TV, the hair dryer, my poor computer. Then they all went off. In the sudden silence, I heard and then saw a small flame lick in and out of an outlet in the sitting room before extinguishing itself.

The fire department came and said that my frayed wiring didn't mix well with my wet walls. I insisted that the owner replace the wiring, which he did, but I never trusted the electric blanket again, even though it wasn't actually the blanket's fault. It went out into the trash.

I complained to my mother that I was using the gas stove again to heat my apartment and running the hair dryer up my shirt to warm my painfully chilled chest. She suggested a hottie. I said no, thanks, my life was complicated enough. This was long before I met Lala. I'd just gotten out of a relationship—I needed a break.

"No, a hot-water bottle. Remember?"

It all came rushing back—I'd almost completely forgotten about her hottie. When I was growing up, my mother boiled water on cold nights and filled her ancient hot-water bottle. I'm not sure how she chose which daughter would use it—she only had one bottle that had to be shared among the three of us. It had a woolen cover, crocheted in what seemed to be leftover yarns in three different colors, and it was tattered-looking, the cover a bit too big for the bottle so that if you weren't careful, the rubber burnt your skin. But it felt special when it was your turn. I was so warm with the bottle at my feet that I tried not to mind the inevitable cold puddle that formed by morning, the water slowly dribbling from the old cracked seal.

"Where do you even *get* one of those?" I asked.

"I got mine in a drugstore in New Zealand thirty-five years ago."

That explained the leaking, I guess. I vowed that as soon as I found out where they were available, I'd buy her a new one.

I went to the Super K-Mart in Oakland, which was one of the few places open twenty-four hours a day. I could go in after my shift at the call center at three in the morning, and shop in a blessedly quiet store, something hard to find in the Bay Area. That night, naturally, I went first to the aisle where electric heating pads were stocked, but no dice. I searched the whole pharmacy without luck. I asked a man who was stocking the shelves if he could help me. While his English was good, I could tell that he'd never run into this particular request before, and I had a hard time explaining it to him. We went back and forth a while until he finally led me to the plungers. I thanked him for his time and drove home, bottle-less.

The next day, I tried Big Longs. Before it was tragically sold in 2010, it was an Oakland paradise. I had a theory that it sold everything—I once bet a friend that it probably sold bindis, the Indian forehead decoration. She said no way. I won the bet and collected happily on my Polish sausage from the hot dog cart, because Big Longs had one of those too. Big Longs sold hats and drugs, booze and socks. They had a full aisle devoted to fly-fishing. They sold fabric *and* yarn. People drove across the Bay Bridge from San Francisco just to visit the gardening department. Big Longs *had* to have a hot-water bottle.

I searched high. I searched low. I enlisted two young men to help me, and they came up empty-handed. Finally, in desperation, I asked the woman at the pharmacy counter if she had any idea where in the world I could find one. She nodded and reached toward a shelf behind her.

"I keep a few back here behind the counter," she explained. "It's not something we normally stock, but I get requests, so I usually have a couple here on special order. Here you go."

She handed me a combo douche and enema kit.

I opened my mouth but it took me a few seconds to compose myself. "No, no," I finally said. "This *looks* like a hot-water bottle, but this is . . ." I lowered my voice to a whisper. "I don't need this stuff." I pointed to the nozzle, hose, and clamp. "I promise, I don't. Not that there's anything wrong with that," I hastened to assure her.

She shrugged. "It's the only way it comes. That's your hot-water bottle. Just throw out the other pieces if you don't want 'em."

I tucked the box under my arm, hoping the print was hidden, and took it to the front register because I had too many other things in my basket to be rung up at the pharmacy. I prayed like I'd never prayed before that the box scanned, that we wouldn't need a price check blared over the PA system.

I made it out alive—no one except the woman behind

me in line saw what I was buying, and she was buying four cans of Raid and a bag of marbles, so I wasn't too concerned with what she thought.

I got home, boiled water, and poured it carefully from my teapot into the mouth of the bottle. Then, of course, I couldn't touch it. Even resting on top of my clothes, it was too hot to use. I thought of the old ratty cover my mother had on hers and knew I needed something like that, a sweater for my bottle. Sure! An easy knitting project: a flat tube, joined in the round, with a doubled-back ribbed collar worked extra long to hide the neck of the bottle. I cast on for it immediately in a blue silk-merino yarn from my stash.

But in the meantime, I still had a hot-water bottle, and my chilly bed was begging for heat. I wrapped the bottle in an old towel and tucked myself up with it. I started with it at my feet, then moved it up as my body warmed until I was hugging it against my chest. Digit fought me for space, curling onto the other side of the bottle. We fell asleep, happy and warm, and when we woke in the morning, the bottle still retained heat.

It was *genius*. How did people not buy these in bulk? Why were they such a secret? I realized that in this respect, I was a late adopter. There was nothing high-tech about a hot-water bottle; you didn't even have to plug it in. And wrapped, as mine would be in a hand-knit cozy, it was so low-tech it was retro.

I finished knitting the cozy. It was just what I wanted, a miniature sweater that hid the rubber bottle (which, despite my best intentions, I kept thinking of as a particu-larly adorable enema bag). I gave it to my mother, who, obviously, had the most need for a new hot-water bottle. She loved it, and in typical Mom fashion, she tucked it carefully into her cedar chest and kept using the old, leaky one with its ancient, ratty cover.

I went back to Big Longs and bought several more enema kits. This time I held my head high. I knew what I was buying was awesome. Four douche/enema kits for me!

The second cozy I made went to a friend who shivered when the temperature dropped below seventy-five, and she, too, fell in love with the usefulness of the gift. We compared notes on how much better our winter sleep was and lamented that so few knew the secret. The third went to a friend whose daughters had both just reached the age of cramps. I told them how much a hottie did to reduce pain, and the next time I got cramps of my own, I thought about them, happy to have been of help.

One night I screeched myself awake when the towel slipped from around the bottle, the rubber burning my stomach. I cast on for another cozy—this one for *me*—in a simple red wool, nice and thick. A night or two in front of the TV watching the one channel it received with its VHF rabbit ears—technologically, I was still stunted on this front—and another hottie sweater was complete. But then it wound up going to a sister who had a birthday coming up. The next, to a friend moving to England.

I wrote up the pattern. As of the date of this writing, years and years later, there are more than 500 people on Ravelry who have made the hot-water bottle cozy, and my favorite email comes from a woman who made one for a teacher on Prince Edward Island, the home of Anne Shirley. It thrilled me to my hand-knit socks to think that something I helped create would make it that far, and the irony that such a low-tech solution made it to the island because the pattern was disseminated in a forum in an online knitting community was not lost on me. It was the perfect marriage of high- and low-tech ingenuity.

Once I was aware of this kind of pairing, I started noticing similarities elsewhere in my household: acoustic instruments paired with digital tuners; an electronic yarn scale next to my spinning wheel; running shoes next to a Garmin GPS watch. Tiny miracles everywhere, but they only felt like miracles if I remained conscious of what came before.

I didn't have a hot-water bottle cozy of my own until my mother died—I found the silk-merino-covered one that she'd carefully stored and I brought it home with me. I've used it a few times, and the smell of cedar that lingers in the wool tugs a place in my heart that aches. Actually, I love the smell so much I keep her bottle in my own cedar chest now. And when I need a hottie, I just boil water and fill the closest hot-water bottle—usually the naked one in the linen cupboard—and wrap an old towel around it. Even simpler than a knitted cozy, it's what I've become used to, and it works for me just fine.

Ten Years Later
I'm happy to report that the hottie has caught on! You can now buy them easily online complete with cute covers, and I've even seen them in physical stores a couple of times. No need for an enema bag, huzzah! My pattern has been made by almost a thousand people, and

the free pattern is at the end of this book. You can see what it looks like at RachaelHerron.com/hottie

I'm warmed to my toes thinking of how much pain or cold each hot water bottle and its cozy might have helped. Do you have one? They're quick and easy to make! Maybe I'll even make one for myself sometime!

REPEAT TO END

$\mathcal{I}$’ve been writing since the day I could hold a pencil. My favorite thing to do when I was a child was hide under my covers and plot books. I wrote my first novel and illustrated it in first grade—it was about a brownie (the fairy kind, not the chocolate kind, although I may have conflated the two: the protagonist had a suspiciously dessert-like shape). And I've been knitting for as long as I've been writing. It took me many years, though, to see that there were more similarities between writing words and knitting stitches than just the fact that I loved doing both.

After I sold my first real, adult novel, I hovered aboveground for a good two months. I wrote a whole book! Holy heck! And a real publisher was going to publish it. It would be in honest-to-God bookstores, and people I wasn't related to would read it. It was a dream come true.

Then, as I realized that I had to write another one, I landed on earth with a painful thud. I'd sold a three-book series, and whenever I mentioned that to other writers, they'd look concerned. "Beware the second-book curse," they intoned, their voices hollow, chains clanking, black cats walking in front of them, and bats flapping past their heads. Okay, that might be a teensy exaggeration, but not much. They tried to scare me, and I tried not to listen.

Because after all, what did I have to worry about? I already had an idea, since I'd had to write several paragraphs on the plots of my upcoming books. I knew the second one would be a romantic suspense, set in the same small town the first novel was set in, and it would be about a bookseller and an ex-cop. The third would be about two doctors, practicing on the same fictional street. What more did I need? It would be great!

Oh, how little did I know. People have different experiences in the writing world, but there's one absolute truth: your second book will kick your ass.

See, there's no pressure on anyone to finish his or her first book. No one is standing at the author's door panting for the first draft of a first novel. I'd had all the time in the world to write my first book because I hadn't sold it yet. There was no deadline, no publisher waiting for me to deliver. It hadn't taken me overly long to write, but I'd had plenty of practice writing: years and years of starting projects, stalling out, starting up again. My second novel, however, was different. I needed to write it in six months, something I'd never done before. No problem, I thought. I'd just bang that puppy out.

During the time I was writing the second book, I was also designing the knitted cardigan pattern that would be included with the book. I wanted it to be very simple and very feminine. I pictured a fitted shape, yellow, with a crocheted, lacy edge. I wasn't sure how I'd design the neck, but I'd figure it out when I got there. It was a bottom-up raglan—no worries.

Oh, how an ego swells before its deflation.

Writing the book was infinitely harder than I thought it would be. I knew it had to be suspenseful, since that's what the publisher had purchased from me, but my characters didn't want to play that way. They were lovey-dovey and they laughed too much; their drama was quirky, not nail-biting. So I threw in a bad guy, made him do some pretty mean things, and then had my heroine shoot him through the heart in the last scene.

Ugh. The suckitude. If I could have admitted to myself that perhaps I'd been writing a mistake of a novel, I would have recognized the problem I was facing. But instead, I just wrote *The End,* and I hoped that while the pages marinated in my closed computer, the manuscript would become good all on its own.

Meanwhile, my knitting pattern was sucking too. I'd made it to the neckline of the bottom-up cardigan, and I had no idea what to do. Whatever I did seemed to go badly, and finally, I just decreased, bound off, and called it good.

But it *wasn't* good. It didn't work. It looked funny when I put it on, all wonky, the collar too tall, the back neckline too short, but I couldn't bear to think about undoing those woven-in ends and ripping back. What was wrong with me? I hadn't made mistakes like this in knitting in ages. I never ripped unless I absolutely had to, and I wasn't willing to admit I'd hit that point.

I sent the manuscript to my agent. Susanna was as kind

as she could be, but over drinks at a conference, she told me the truth. The novel wasn't working. I heard it, knew she was right, and started to panic.

"Crap," I said, knitting furiously away on a sock. At least I knew how to make those.

She nodded and said nothing.

"How do I fix it?"

"Can you. . .? Um . . ." She looked up at the skylight. Usually excellent at brainstorming, she was at a loss. So Susanna did something that agents do and writers often don't: she called my editor, who was attending the same conference. May bounced down on her way to the gym, looking adorable and tiny. I felt like the Incredible Hulk next to her as I screwed up every ounce of courage I had and said all in one breath, "What if I rewrote my book and made it women's fiction? With no suspense." I closed my eyes and waited for the blow.

It didn't come. May said, "Okay."

"Excuse me?"

"Whatever you want. Just write what the story needs."

I collapsed in a grateful heap before I realized that I'd just agreed to revise my novel. And it wasn't a small edit, adding a few things or taking away others—it was going to be a total rewrite, from beginning to end, and it was due in eight weeks. I started to sweat in the cool lobby. Then I wondered how the hell one really revised.

In my hotel room, instead of turning on my computer, I picked up the yellow sweater I'd brought with me. I tried it on again and, just like before, it looked wrong. I took a deep breath and sat in front of the window in the hotel armchair. I started unraveling the sweater.

For the next two months, I pulled apart the novel and put it back together again, and, at the same time, I reworked the whole sweater. I finished the rewrite and turned it in. While I waited to hear from my editor, I finished the sweater. It turned out okay. I didn't love the way the shoulders lay, but I didn't hate it. It was kind of wearable. Mostly.

While I wondered whether I was up for ripping the yarn out again, I got a call from May. I stood in a parking lot holding my cell phone, trying to keep my hands from shaking as she told me, "Your writing is strong and so are your characters. But you need a plot." Her voice was kind. She'd done this before with second novels.

"Can I fix it?" I needed reassurance. I wanted her to say, *Of course. No problem.*

"Well, it's going to take some heavy lifting," she said.

I sat on the curb, feeling like I'd been sucker-punched. No plot? Of course I had plot! The characters got totally mad at each other! You know . . . they were really mad . . . so mad . . . oh crap. She was right. I had emotional conflict, essential to a good romance plot, but since I'd taken the ridiculous bad guy out, I had nothing that couldn't be solved with a fifteen-minute heart-to-heart discussion. That wasn't real conflict, that was just a bad mood.

And now I loved the book too much to scrap it. I had one more shot, and I had to nail it. I packed my car with the damn manuscript, the damn yellow sweater, and a couple bottles of wine, and drove to Pigeon Point, a hostel on the coast an hour south of San Francisco where my fictional town was set. I got a private room—from the bed I could see the base of the decrepit lighthouse. I stared at it, waiting for a breakthrough. Where was my inspiration? I was ready for it. Come on, dammit!

I wore the sweater as I walked past the lighthouse and down to the beach at sunset, and I pulled at the neck, trying to make the collar and shoulders fit better. I continued waiting, as the sun dove into the sea, turning the sand golden on the beach. I was the only person in sight. I waited for my own illumination. I knew from movies that because I was at my lowest, the answer was just around the corner. Any second now, Morgan Freeman would rise from behind a rock and say something Godlike, and I'd know how to fix the novel. If I were really lucky, he might dispense knitting advice too.

It didn't happen. The sun disappeared, and I got cold, and the light of the auto-strobe at the base of the defunct lighthouse blinded me so that I tripped as I felt my way up the cliff toward the hostel, skinning my knee. In my room, I looked at the words I'd written, and I still didn't know what to do. In the same way I knew what shape I wanted the sweater to take, I knew how I wanted the novel to hang together. I knew what I wanted it to say in the end—I just didn't know how to get there.

In the shared kitchen of the hostel, a woman put a chicken into the oven for dinner. As she wandered away, I asked, "How long are you going to cook it for?" I had my manuscript spread out on the kitchen table and wanted to know when I'd have to move.

She looked at me in surprise and said, "I don't know. I just let it cook till it's done."

I'm pretty sure Morgan Freeman wouldn't be caught

dead in the broomstick skirt she was wearing, and it wasn't exactly instruction from the divine. It was cooking advice from a woman visiting from Iowa. But it was what I needed.

I turned to the front page and started working. Again. The book would be done when it was done, and if I didn't know how to get there, I'd figure it out on the way. I lifted paragraphs and moved them. Inspiration came in painful flashes, like the lighthouse's beam. I shifted whole chapters, moving and rearranging, adding and subtracting. At the same time, I ripped back the sweater again too, starting from the sleeves, trusting my hands to knit it new, knit it better.

In take three, I finally understood: revision is as creative a process as writing the first draft. The reason the later draft is better is because it rests on the bones of the drafts below it, even if it's unrecognizable from its earlier forms. In life, if one makes a mistake, it may be permanent. A broken glass remains a broken glass—you're unlikely to put it back together. But in both knitting and writing, mistakes can be made, learned from, and unmade, in order to make something new, something better.

I added the hostel's lighthouse to my book, making it an essential part of the plot. I added a long collar to the cardigan, something it took me a while to realize it needed. The book I ended up with is exactly what I wanted, even though I didn't know it until I was done. The yellow cardigan fits me perfectly. And I'm less nervous now than I used to be, in both knitting and writing, which is to say, in my life.

At least while knitting and writing—those two essential parts of who I am—I can always go back and fix things. I know how. It makes me bold. And it's a comfort to know that when I knit badly or when I write poorly, I haven't really lost anything but time—and even that time has changed into something: knowledge. Every time I fail, it hurts like hell. But I know more than I did before I tried.

And knitters are a hardy lot, aren't we? We keep clicking along, one stitch following another, mistakes noticed and often fixed. We keep going, just as writers keep putting words on the page, whether we're filling journals or writing novels. As the Yarn Harlot, Stephanie Pearl-McPhee, has said, small actions, repeated over and over, lead to astonishingly large results—stitches become sweaters, words become books. Many knitters added together become a community. And we're here for each other when it's hard, with plenty of yarn to share.

Ten Years Later
Boy, I've written a lot of books since then, writing actively in five genres: memoir, commercial upmarket fiction, thriller, romance, and nonfiction about writing. And I still finish at least one or two sweaters a year, with four or five pairs of socks and a shawl sneaking in every once in a while. Writing and knitting are still my life, and I'm happy to say I love revision so much that I teach it.

We take our best stabs at things, and if we're being brave and acting out of courage, not fear, we will fail. I fail all the time! I fail at making my books say what I want them to in the first draft, or even in the fourth draft, sometimes. Failure is a huge part of my writing (and my knitting) journey, and thank goodness for it. Like the Japanese proverb says, it's about getting up just one more time than you fall. That's all that matters.

DUPLICATE STITCH

$\mathcal{A}$s a child, I begged to be told stories of my mother's youth, about teaching in Europe, or living in Samoa, anything at all about her glamorous, pre-mother life. The fact that she'd had such a different life before us fascinated me as a child. I stole peeks at her photo albums whenever she would let me—they showed pictures of her at parties in Germany in which she looks like a glamorous extra on the set of *Mad Men.* Very young, beautiful men were draped over settees in low light, sitting next to women with long, fringed lashes and high, coiffed hair. All of them smoked and held highballs in their hands, and all of them smiled.

She didn't tell us many stories, but I knew one. While traveling near the fjords of Norway in her early twenties, she met a woman who knitted sweaters to order. The woman measured my mother and told her to come back in a month. My mother returned, and the sweater, a traditional Setesdal cardigan worked in a dark mossy green background with cream contrasting stitches, fit her perfectly.

Good, strong, overspun wool, it was knit at a tight gauge and wore like iron. After forty years of use, Mom had only worn a few holes in it at the turned cuff of the sleeve and at the hem, easily fixable.

I loved that sweater. She put it away with the winter clothes at the first sign of spring, and when she pulled it out of the box in fall, it was a sure sign that the rains were coming. It was the sweater she wore when the kitchen was cold in the mornings. She wore it with her good jeans when she went out at night with my father, rare and strange occasions when she put on lipstick and transformed into someone we barely knew. On the couch at night, in front of the fire, Mom cradled us in her arms, and I have vivid memories of tracing the peeries with my fingers as she read. I loved nothing more than falling asleep to the sound of her voice reading to us, my head on her shoulder, my hand on her wrist, still touching the wool.

The sweater was part of my history, but it never really struck me until I was an adult that it was hand-knit. It was so far beyond anything I'd ever be able to do. I was only an American knitter (even though I held the yarn with my left hand, using a modified throwing style). But her sweater was *Norwegian*, the pinnacle of knitted accomplishment.

I knitted for years and years without much confidence in my ability. I knew I could read patterns and follow them, but they felt like recipes—I wouldn't dare make bread without consulting the cookbook, and I wouldn't dare cast on without someone else telling me how many stitches to place on my needle unless it was for something very simple.

But always, in the back of my mind, there was the thought that someday, if I got good enough, maybe I'd be able to find a pattern that replicated parts of Mom's sweater. Maybe I'd get good enough to attempt something that kind of looked like hers. Perhaps I'd match the color of the yarns. A Dale of Norway kit, maybe, would be a good place to start. I knew, obviously, I'd never find the exact sweater, with its intricate designs and small motifs, but many Setesdals looked similar to hers, and whenever I saw a woman on the street wearing one, I was always hit with an inappropriate urge to hug her.

Then, when I was thirty-five, my little mama got sick. She'd been sick before with multiple large, scary illnesses: sarcoidosis, colon cancer. But even though she was small, she was strong. A fighter. Healthy. She fought things off with a will as strongly spun as the wool in her Norse sweater, and she usually swept disease out of her body like she swept dirt out of her house. Nothing a little scrubbing wouldn't fix.

This sickness, though, was something different. No one knew what was wrong. She got weaker. Unable to stop losing weight, she got smaller. I smothered her with kisses, which she batted away like an annoyed cat, but I saw the smile she couldn't hide as she turned away. She called me ridiculous, and I knew it was a compliment.

One day, I took down the green sweater from the top shelf of her closet and draped it on the kitchen table. I was only looking for inspiration, something I could search for on Ravelry.

But instead, I saw something else, and I sat heavily in Dad's creaky cane chair at the head of the table.

"I can make this," I said, shocked.

Mom put the kettle on for a cup of tea. "But why would you?"

"Because I can."

"Someday you can just have that one."

I hated what her words implied, and they left me speechless.

She went on, "Besides, you knit sweaters that are so much nicer than that old thing."

The excitement rose again. "But I could do it."

I ran my fingers over it, turning it over, pulling the seams apart gently, peering into its workings. "Do you have graph paper?"

Bless her, of course she did. It must have been left over from when she'd home-schooled us overseas, more than twenty years before, but she knew exactly where it was. I started charting out the graphs, my pencil scribbling against paper on top of the kitchen table, where I'd done hundreds of hours of homework in my teens.

Now I was doing the most exciting homework of my life. Why hadn't I figured out earlier that sweater deconstruction was just math? I would have reknitted a million of my favorite sweaters had I known that! I figured out the gauge, measured how wide it was (it had fit me perfectly since I stopped growing, just like it did Mom), and started jotting numbers. Mom pulled up a chair and laughed as my pencil practically smoked against the paper.

"I can *do* this."

She nodded. "I never doubted it."

I took my chicken-scratch notes and the graph paper and drove northward home, where I ordered dark green and cream Jamieson's Spindrift. It was a much lighter-weight yarn than that used in Mom's heavy sweater, but I wanted something that I'd be able to wear in California and also still achieve gauge with my loose hand.

Not long after ordering the yarn, I had a difficult conversation with Mom over the phone. She'd sounded confused and upset, two things my mother never was. Almost as upsetting, she was also at times perfectly clear. She was cognizant that something was happening to her, and that it was unpleasant, and that she couldn't remember or figure out what it was. It was the saddest I'd ever heard her sound.

I made my voice happy. I laughed. "I'll kiss Digit so *hard* for you, he'll growl in your direction." My obstreperous cat loved very few people, but my mother was one of them. "I love you," I said cheerfully.

"I love you too." Her voice broke. I lived only five hours away from her, but with work and obligations and life, she felt so much farther away.

The yarn arrived quickly. As I pulled it from its box, I decided that it was almost perfect. Not quite the same green as Mom's, but it would do. I sat on the couch and pulled out my notes. I cast on for the sleeve. I turned on a stupid TV reality show and didn't watch—instead I looked at my hands working the twisted rib cuff. It went faster than I'd thought it would, and soon I was picking up the first ball of cream to start the first motif. Since it was around the wrist, it also went quickly, and before I knew it, the first two peeries were done.

I slid it onto my wrist to check the size, the circular needle cold at my forearm.

It was as if my mother's arm were right there, coming around me. For a single, jolted second, my adult eyes changed into those of a child, and I remembered, vividly, what it felt like to sit in my mother's lap, her arms around me, my hands resting on top of her sleeve, my fingers running up and down the cream stitches, jogging up the design, tapping each V, practicing counting by figuring out how many cream stitches fit between the motifs.

I was knitting my mother's arms around me. The images on the television swam in my tear-filled eyes.

Months later, I finished the sweater at her bedside in Arroyo Grande Hospital. The word *hospice* had just been uttered for the first time, and instead of processing what that meant to my family, I sewed on pewter buttons as if my life depended on it. Or rather, as if *her* life depended on it. Those buttons, sewn on with desperation and all the hope my lungs could breathe in my mother's direction, wouldn't ever be removable except possibly with a pry bar. Thank God I put them in the right place.

By then, she was too tired to read. Finally diagnosed with multiple myeloma, she only had a few weeks left. The manuscript of my first novel, still unsold at that point, sat in a binder next to her. I read her the first few pages before she was too tired to listen, and then I stood outside the hospital, my forehead pressed into the concrete wall, tears streaming down my face.

My little mama would never read my book.

My biggest champion, the woman who had always believed the most in me and in my dream of being a writer, even during the dark moments when I'd given it up, would never live to see it carried out.

The pain was unbearable and, at the same time, I'd never felt more selfish. What did my book matter when my mother was dying? I rubbed my face on my T-shirt and lifted my face to the sun.

Inside, I wove in the final ends. Mom was sleeping again. As I snipped the last bit of yarn, the moment was anticlimactic. But as if she heard it, Mom's eyes opened. I shook the sweater out and held it up.

"Hey, Mom, look. I finished the replica of your sweater."

She smiled weakly. "Oh, good."

"Isn't it pretty? Look," I shrugged it on. "It fits!"

"It looks so nice. . . May I . . . have some water?"

I reached to do the things I'd been doing for weeks, giving her a bit of Ensure, coaxing her to take a bite of the awful coagulated pudding, all while wearing my new sweater. I didn't even consider wrapping Mom in hers, which I'd brought with me with the hope of taking photos in our twin sweaters. It would have been too difficult to move her.

But later, when my sisters had gone to find food and Dad had gone back to the house to feed the cats, I sat at the edge of her bed and read a few more of my unpublished book's pages to her until she fell asleep.

Then I leaned forward and held her, and the same patterns and motifs that had encircled me, keeping me safe all my life, now held my little mama. She slept, her head on my shoulder, her hand on my wrist.

BLANKET STITCH

I wish you could see the Love Blanket that the knitters who read my blog made me when Mom died. I wish you could run your fingers over the squares countless times like I have. Every time I do, I find something new to marvel at. Rachel M and Dani knitted the same Tree of Life but in different colors. They flank a heart done by Lyssa. Jove made stripes. Eleanor's square came all the way from Britain. Rachel T used handspun, saffron-dyed Blue Faced Leicester, and Michelle knitted her square on the anniversary of her mother's death.

I can't tell you about every square in my blanket, because it would take too long, but let me tell you about Celia's. Celia is a friend in real life, as well as a blogging buddy. For years, my sister Christy had said, "You *have* to meet this woman I work with. She knits like you do, like a bat out of woolly hell." Celia was, indeed, one of my clan. She wore her brightly colored knits with joy, and hugged with abandon. The square she made was red and had four pink hearts. One extra pink heart floated above the others and boasted small white wings. It wasn't even until I was writing my blog post about the blanket that I realized that the top heart was my little mama, the other four were my father, my two sisters, and me. My heart broke clean open.

The blanket's creation was a big internet secret, one that Lala knew about and successfully kept from me. One evening she came home from work with a large box with my name on it and just shook her head and grinned when I asked her what was going on. I opened the flaps and pulled out my Love Blanket.

Composed of more than fifty knitted squares, each one completely different from its neighbor, it was seamed in black, which gave the back a stained-glass effect. I knew this kind of blanket, had read about them online, had in fact contributed to the construction of several over the years, but I'd never seen one in person before. It quite literally took my breath away. I felt like the air had been sucked out of the room, and I had to concentrate on taking my next breath, pulling the suddenly thin air into my lungs.

People had cared enough to do this for me. For me.

Inside the box was also a red fabric bag filled with handwritten notes from the knitters, personal notes of love and loss, kindness and grace. Emily's read, "Mine is the one made of custom green-and-purple silk/wool yarn. It's the one in the middle. It's not a fancy stitch pattern like some of the others, but every stitch was knit with your peace of heart in mind."

When I asked Krista Moore, the driving force behind the blanket, why she'd been moved to put it together for me, she said that her own mother was "a beacon in my life, and I could tell you felt the same way about your own mother. When you shared your sad news with us, I fell to pieces. I could feel your heartbreak because it was too close to home. I had to do something, I had to hug you and kiss you on the cheek and tell you, *We are sisters, you and I. I know your pain and I grieve with you.* If I could have gone weeks without sleep and knit you that whole blanket I would have, but I knew that there were so many more who felt the same way as I did. I knew that if I sent up the Bat-Signal, the response would be overwhelming. And it was."

She gave those who responded her address and a deadline. The only rule was that the square had to be eight by eight inches. When they arrived at her house, she started seaming them all together with a simple crocheted edge. Her life was suddenly complicated when her young, healthy brother suffered a stroke, and she said, "The best help I could offer my family was to babysit my brother's infant, so while Cale slept, I laid out your squares and began to join them. Your blanket became my therapy too. I prayed for you, your sisters, your dad, my brother, his children. The prayers flew out of me. I knew there was more love in that blanket than I had ever felt before when I packed it up and sent it on its way."

By the time I received it, her brother was healing and, astonishingly, with the blanket wrapped around me, I found that my healing had also begun.

I swear I didn't go out and look for someone I could direct my karmic abundance toward, but within six months, I found a reason to give a blanket forward. In the course of four short months, a Canadian knitter named Zoom had seriously injured her back, lost her job of eighteen years, and was diagnosed with breast cancer.

I'd virtually "met" Zoom through my online friend Grace. No, scratch that last adjective. Grace is a *real* friend, one that I made because I wrote a blog she liked, and because her comments have always meant a lot to me. I haven't met her in person, but we've emailed frequently and talked on the phone, and when her cat, Ramona, died, I cried almost as hard as if Ramona had been my own. At some point in our friendship, Grace told me I should be reading Zoom. She was right—I loved Zoom's humor, fearlessness, and, not least of all, her orange cat, Duncan, who was the size of a beer truck.

Grace, being very Grace, shot me a quick Facebook note saying that Zoom could use some love. I clicked over to Zoom's blog, where I learned about her cancer diagnosis. Two weeks later, I sent Grace a message asking if she'd help me make a blanket for her. She loved the idea as I knew she would, and I spent hours trolling Zoom's blog, pulling up likely looking comments, sending their authors queries, and getting the plan in place.

And then we knitted. I loved sitting on my couch in Oakland, California, thinking about the knitters all over the world, knitting at the same time, putting prayers and good wishes into each careful stitch. Grace collected the Canadian squares; I received the Stateside ones. All told, we collected squares from four countries: the United States, Canada, Sudan, and Australia. It got so that I couldn't wait for the mail to come—I'd run out and have the packages half open by the time I got inside. "Ooh!" I'd cry. "Look at this one! It has a whole garden on it. Oh! It's Zoom's community garden! There are her carrots!" After the deadline, Grace posted the Canadian squares to me, and when I received them, unpacking the box felt as joyous as unwrapping birthday presents.

Krista had sewn together all the squares on my Love Blanket by herself. I sat in my house surrounded by dozens of squares, thinking about that much crochet. I didn't even try to do the math to figure out how many years it would take me. I knew I wasn't woman enough to handle it by myself. I called in the troops.

Friends and family gathered one Saturday afternoon in an updated version of a quilting bee. Just as communities of women used to gather over a quilting frame to quilt, we gathered with a singular purpose, first at our computers and later to sew each loving square into one blanket. I felt connected to generations before me as I realized that my Love Blanket was the result of another bee in another place, and I knew I was extraordinarily lucky.

Our table groaned under the weight of the goodies. Annie brought cookies and three kinds of delicious-smelling handmade soap that her mother-in-law made. Rachel M, who had contributed to my blanket, brought cookies and spare crochet hooks. Courtney brought her amazing laugh. Janine, the woman who taught me to spin, came. Even my sisters were there, ready to help. None of them were readers of Zoom's blog, so while we sat on the floor and crocheted the squares together, I told stories of her life, and if I'd stopped to think, *These are just stories I read online, you don't really know this woman,* I would have stuttered to a stop.

I believe I do know Zoom, in the way that she lets me know her: online. So many times, I've met readers of my blog who say things like, "I feel like I know you. I know that's weird, I'm sorry," before they back away, blushing. But it's not weird. It's true. My readers do know me, and I know an astonishing number of them too. Of course, I don't put everything on the blog—I couldn't. The way in which I share my life online is exactly the same as the way I share my life in person: I tell select stories of my choosing, just as we all do. Filters are different in different situations, and interestingly, I often tell stories online that I don't tell anywhere else. It's an intimate space, and I know my readers are listening and remembering, creating a deep well of collective memory and incredible kindness.

I mailed the blanket to Grace and she delivered the blanket in person to Zoom. The next morning, I got an email from Zoom that read, "I woke up in the middle of the night and just lay there thinking about it for a long time. About how such a freakishly bad year has been so deeply good in so many ways. About how terrified and alone I felt in the beginning, and how safe and nurtured I feel now, and how much of that I owe to the knitters and bloggers of the world. I thought about the process that went into this blanket, and the community and the symbolism, and about how friends I've never even met could care so much about me that they would somehow get together and transcend geography to make me something so wonderful and heart-warming and nurturing and full of love. . . If there's a fire, it'll be the thing I save."

I feel the same way about my Love Blanket. After people and pets, I'd save it first. It lives on my writing chair in my office. I didn't want the blanket to go on the bed— the dogs would sleep on it, and it would get dirty from everyday use. Instead, I stow it in plain sight while still keeping it safe, and I can't count the number of times I've been in my office on cold mornings when I've dragged the blanket over my shoulders, wrapping it around myself, piling the extra in my lap. Or how often I've sat in the soft chair revising with the wool draped over me. Cats struggle to sit on my lap, but I don't let them share with me often. This is the most special blanket in my house, the most perfect weapon in my war on grief. It edges everything out for the sheer love in every single square inch. I can feel the kindness in it. Only a small percentage of my online friends contributed to the actual blanket itself, but the stitches carry the weight of all the others. I hope that Zoom feels the same way with her blanket. They're literal representations of love, grace, and kindness. You can roll your eyes at me, but I think my blanket might be made of magic.

And it's so warm, too.

Ten Years Later
Eventually, I got lazy and started leaving the Love Blanket on the wee couch in my writing office. I loved that it was always close to hand, but so did the animals. Pets are hard on blankets. Clara loved to groan her border collie way onto it and bury her nose under a soft fold. Both Miss Idaho and Dozy would try to dig into it with their front paws to make a perfect nest—I never let them do it when I was in my office, but I wasn't always there.

Recently, as we prepped for our move to New Zealand, I held the blanket up and counted up the tragic holes, all of which I could be blamed for. *What was I thinking? I should have made sure no animal ever touched it. I should have stored it away somewhere, safe.* I spent hours beating myself up, and then suddenly realized something obvious. I could just fix the holes.

I've darned plenty of things, but all of them garments. (Never socks—for those, I take Stephanie Pearl-McPhee's approach of saying "Oh, darn," as I drop them in the trash bin.) I'm a huge fan of the visiblemending hashtag on Instagram, and I love fixing holes in my sweaters with contrasting bits of yarn. But the rips and tears on the blanket were bigger than the small holes I'd worn in my sweaters.

There had to be a way, and yep, thanks to YouTube, I learned how to pick up and knit from below a hole and knit a patch to cover each one. I used only my own handspun, intending to keep each knitted square filled with love.

When I finished patching, I folded up the blanket and packed it carefully in the cedar hope chest. I hear it gets cold in New Zealand in winter. I'm not scared.

DRAFTING TRIANGLE

*W*hen I was perhaps twenty-seven, I visited my parents' home, and while I knitted in the living room, I listened to my mother humming along with the old songs on her radio. Arlo Guthrie's classic "City of New Orleans" came on, and she moved from humming to singing quietly along with every word. My eyes welled with tears, as they always did when I heard a snippet of that song—no matter where I was, in a campground listening to a stranger play it on his beat-up guitar or skimming over radio stations while driving up the Central Valley, I always experienced an emotional surge that I never saw coming.

I wandered into the kitchen, dabbing at my eyes with my sleeve. "I wonder why I cry whenever I hear this song?" Embarrassed, I reached for a Kleenex.

My mother stopped moving and stared at me. "Do you remember?"

I frowned and shook my head.

"Of course you wouldn't remember, but this was our

song. I put it on the record player and danced you to sleep to this every night when you were a baby."

I stood there, stunned, as I *almost* remembered the feeling of her rocking me to sleep. I wished for that memory, longed for it, knowing a memory like that could get someone through just about anything.

It seems almost unbelievable to me that my mother never forgot anything, and seemed to know a little something about positively everything. But I wasn't alone in thinking this about her. I worked with her at a bookstore for years, and I watched the residents of our small town come to the store just to ask her questions. This was before the internet, and instead of going to the library, customers visited Jan. "When is the next gibbous moon?" "How do you make a battery?" "Where's Belarus?" She was like a walking encyclopedia, and I used to field the phone calls of customers who were disappointed when she wasn't working. And no, I didn't have the answer, sorry.

Mom knew odd things. Things no one else knew. Sometimes I worry that with my famously bad memory, I'll someday forget the things that are most important to remember. I don't need the eight times table (God knows I've only barely known it at the best of times), but what if I forget how to knit? What would that feel like, to sit with sticks and string and not know what to do with them? It would be like forgetting how to use a language, I think.

And sometimes I believe the harder I try to hold things in my memory, the faster they fall out. The tighter my grasp, the less I retain. I forget names and dates. I forget to pick up the mail and to feed the dogs and, worse, I've forgotten plans, not showing up where I'm supposed to be because I'm so forgetful, still knitting in front of the TV, unaware I've let anyone down. After twenty-five years of trying, I finally remember how to start the Kitchener stitch, but I have as slippery a hold on the concept as I do the eight times table.

But after some trial and error, I've come up with what I think is a clever way of coping with this problem since my mother, The One Who Knew, died. It's this: I find smart, kind women who remind me of her, and I befriend them. Now, I know some women don't have mentors. They don't need them, perhaps. They are content with friends, coworkers, peers. But having had such a remarkable woman to look up to all my life has conditioned me to want more than just that, if I can get it.

I don't think the women I've picked for this role in my life really know I'm making surrogate mothers of them, but because they are who they are, they won't mind when they read this and find out—each one is maternal enough to love me anyway, even though none of them are old enough to actually be my mother. Sophie Littlefield will laugh and call me darling and make me feel like I'm the center of the universe and that everything I say is the smartest thing that's ever been said. Barbara Bretton will send me an email when she reads this, but what she won't know is that it will catch me exactly at the moment I'm falling, about to face-plant on the concrete—her words will cushion me from hitting the bottom. Esther Luevano, who at first glance might come off as a softie, doesn't take any crap from anyone anymore, and she'll let me baby her if I want to, the way I used to baby my little mama—she'll let me worry about her and tell her to rest and insist she needs another cup of tea, and she gives me kisses when I cry.

And then there's Janine Bajus.

Janine came into my life when she moved to the Bay Area from Seattle. My friend Ryan sent me an email that said: "The Feral Knitter is moving. She won't know anyone, and I think you two should meet." We've all had these kinds of emails before—friend, meet friend! Everyone is cc'd, everyone writes back: "Yes, lunch some-time!" And then the common decency box is checked off, and if you forget to get back in touch, no one's feelings are hurt.

But the Feral Knitter (so-called because a friend misun-derstood the words "Fair Isle Knitter" and the misnomer stuck) was different. Something in her email made me suggest a knitting coffee date. We met for the first time at the Temescal Café on Telegraph Avenue, just doors down from my favorite knitting shop. And over coffee and easy laughter, I decided on the spot to adopt a new friend. Whether she liked it or not, I was keeping her. It was the nicest friend blind date I'd ever been on.

There's just something about Janine—please pardon my French—that precludes the bullshit. With her blunt-cut shoulder-length brown hair and bangs, open smile, and the way that she really *looks* at you when you talk, she leaves you one option: you tell her the truth. And if you don't know the truth, you think about it and figure it out while you're talking to her, and she'll make a connection to something else in your life, something you never thought of but should have.

And she knows her knitting. She's my knit-guru, my

personal Elizabeth Zimmerman. She came up with—get this—set-in sleeve caps that are worked in the round. (Knitters: I know. Non-knitters, or new knitters: trust me, this means she's a genius.) She taught me how to spin one afternoon, and we were, that afternoon, part of a line of women dating back thousands of years. My mother didn't spin—probably one of the few things she didn't know how to do—so she'd never taught me. Janine's daughter knitted, but didn't yet spin or show an inclination to do so.

As she taught me, we wondered how many women had sat together spinning, just like this: one patient, the other frustrated. In that moment, we symbolized mother and daughter throughout the ages. Janine, of course, was the one who commented on it that afternoon. I was too busy swearing at the wheel to notice it until she did, and if I painted the air blue with curse words, she was genteel enough not to comment on them, to wait until the air cleared before she spoke again, just as my mother would have.

I adopted Janine as my friend and mentor before my mother died, and while I didn't do it consciously, I was so lucky that she was there for me afterward. When I got word that my book had sold, Janine was the second person I told, after I'd woken up Lala. Janine got the first galley of my first novel, the one Mom would have received.

Since Janine taught me to spin before Mom died, I brought the spinning wheel to our family campsite at bluegrass festivals. In the past, while people played guitars and fiddles, I'd keep time with my foot on the treadle, playing my own tune. Mom even tried it once, with my hands guiding hers, and she was a natural spinner, of course. It didn't surprise me.

One of those festival nights, Mom and I sat watching Arlo Guthrie on the main stage. The meadow grew dark as he sang, and the sky above us sparked with falling stars. He sang "City of New Orleans," and my mother and I held hands until the song was done. She'd been diagnosed with cancer, and was heading into surgery the next week. We both knew it might be the last time we'd ever hear him sing us our song.

It was.

Years later, I stood in the same meadow, watching Arlo again, and closed my eyes as he sang, *Mothers with their babes asleep, Are rockin' to the gentle beat, And the rhythm of the rails is all they feel.* I grieved, tears coursing down my face in the dark, but underneath, I felt buoyed by the knowledge that I will never, ever forget why that song makes me cry. And no matter how bad I do get at remembering, I hold a brightly colored, handspun, knitted ace in the hole: a repository of stored memory, held by my friends. And I hope I provide, every once in a while, a shoulder—and a memory—for them to lean on, too.

LIFELINE

This essay is specially written just for this tenth anniversary edition.

Six or seven years ago, I bought mink yarn in Iceland.

The store owner lowered her voice as I put it on her counter. "It isn't vegan," she said, her eyes wide. "Is that okay?"

"I'm not a vegan. I like animal yarns, that's okay," I assured her. The two balls were the shade of the tundra outside, verdant greens and yellows tumbled with marshy browns and grays. Rather than being the dreary color of an old bruise as one might have thought, the shades burst with life, exactly mimicking the hues of the moss that clung to the cold lava flows of the Icelandic terrain. The moss and lichen bound the soil and prevented sand drift, so it was protected, which meant that even though I'd longed to fall against the springy-looking stuff we kept driving past, I knew I couldn't. This incredibly soft yarn would be my substitute, as close as I would get to rubbing my face against the landscape.

It wasn't until that night, in our snug little house in Reykjavik, that I Googled minks. Oh, son of a biscuit. Not only was the yarn not vegan, it seemed the little critters were raised and killed for their coats. Ack. Was I a monster? I poured myself another glass of wine and petted the yarn, thanking the vicious little predator for its existence, trying to assuage my guilt by imagining what a soft shawl it would make. But I felt badly enough about it that I didn't cast on immediately, as I'd planned. I tucked it into my suitcase and went about trying to see the Northern Lights. After spending many happy hours in as many community "hot pots" as we could find—our favorite was Björk's local hot spring, though we are sad to report we never saw her or the Northern Lights—we went home, where I stuck the mink yarn in the "special" basket.

You probably have one of those baskets yourself. And sure, let's imagine that we only have one each, shall we? I appreciate the kindness of this lie. Of course, I'm talking about the basket that holds the impulse buys you can't let go: the cashmere you couldn't afford more than one ball of but like to pet on blue days, the incredible hand painted superwash merino a friend made for you in your favorite colors, the single hank of raw Habu silk that you know you'll never use but like to juggle from hand to hand every once in a while.

That's where the mink lived. It would have been happy to linger there with its oddball, pretty friends for a long time, but one day, I needed it. Badly.

Because no one plans to get sober nine days before traveling alone to Spain.

In case you're going to Spain, I can't make this more clear: I do not recommend quitting drinking less than two weeks before going to the Land of Sangria. Exceedingly poor planning on my part. And it was all thanks to the morning pages.

Do you know about Julia Cameron's morning pages from her classic book, *The Artist's Way*? She encourages you to write three longhand pages as soon as you wake up. The morning pages are not "good" writing—in fact, they're barely even journaling. The thoughts at the top of your mind fall out and onto the page, and most of the time those thoughts are pretty banal. I spend a lot of time planning work and grocery shopping in mine, truly scintillating work. But regularly enough to be predictable, a major revelation will smack you in the face, a revelation that might have stayed hidden had you not been writing every day.

One cold February morning, after doing a session of yoga on YouTube in which the instructor asked us to really hear our hearts, my heart responded by saying something incredibly rude. I turned to my desk and wrote it down in my morning pages.

I am an alcoholic.

Well, shit.

I was really good at writing about how I *wasn't* one. I'd been doing that for months. Years, perhaps. Many many pages of *I can't be an alcoholic because I've never gotten in trouble for drinking too much. I can't be an alcoholic because I've never hit rock bottom. I can't be an alcoholic because I have a great wife, an awesome house, loving friends, and money in the bank.* I think it's pretty safe to say that no one journals as much I did about how they don't have a drinking problem unless they do, in fact, have a big old problem.

That day, though, I wrote the truth.

I am an alcoholic.

I sat and gawped at the sentence for a while, thinking if I were normal, I'd probably cry at the revelation. Instead, I felt a certain detached numbness and a jolt of bone-deep truth that made my skin give an all-over twinge.

Then I did what I do—faced with a problem that suddenly had a name, I set about finding a fix. I Googled Alcoholics Anonymous.

I was in a meeting two hours later.

For the next eight days in a row, I stepped across the threshold of anonymity and into the laughter of people living a much freer life than the one I'd been muddling through. (Speaking of that anonymity, the only rule for membership in AA is that you have the desire to stop drinking. The tradition of not speaking about the secret society is one I knowingly choose to break on the off chance someone reads this who might benefit from hearing about the help I found.)

Those meetings quickly became a lifeline. I'd been drinking since I was in my early twenties, and I didn't know how to exist as an adult without my wine. The members there knew not only how to exist but how to *thrive*. I wanted what they had.

At the last meeting I attended before I got on the plane for Spain, I told the group that I was leaving the country the next day to be alone in a wine-drenched country. "I don't know how I'm going to make it." A soft, unintelligible murmur moved around the room, and after the meeting, I found myself surrounded by friendly, cheerful women.

"Get the Meeting Guide app. It'll show you where all the English-speaking meetings are." I hadn't even considered that there might be meetings in English for me to attend.

"Keep your twenty-four-hour chip in your purse." My purse? I'd had that sucker in my bra for eight days, pressed against my heart. I needed it closer than just my bag.

"Take my phone number. Text or call me anytime." My phone filled with numbers I knew I'd be too shy to use.

"Carry something to fiddle with everywhere you go." SOMETHING TO FIDDLE WITH? Hey! Hold up!

I knew *all* about fiddling!

Why hadn't I thought of knitting? It had gotten me through quitting smoking—could knitting be strong enough to help this time?

I'd been in a knitting slump so heavy my shoulders drooped with it. That said, I'd just been in a slump, period, for almost a year, as my drinking had gotten rapidly heavier. This was literally life and death—I knew I couldn't hold things together much longer. Everything had been affected, although so far only in ways that I could see. To be very clear: no one knew I was an alcoholic, not even my wife. I was so very good at hiding it. I carefully timed my passing out from white wine to bedtime, toppling over as if exhausted, when it was really the alcohol pulling down my eyelids and sending me unconscious. I didn't over-drink when I was out with friends, out of concern that they'd figure it out. One of my friends got sloppy when she drank too much, and I hated seeing her that way because I knew I was an inch from being that person myself.

Rigid control was all I had left—I *had* to hold everything together, and I did, by the skin of my teeth. My drinking didn't affect my ability to meet publishing deadlines. I never lost a job. I never crashed a car. I didn't lose any relationships. But deep down I knew I was in imminent danger of losing *myself* to this thing that was getting stronger than me by the day. In those first eight meetings, I was just starting to see that there might be hope. There might be light, even though I didn't know if I could stand the brightness.

Desperately, I downloaded the meeting app. I made sure my twenty-four-hour chip was always pressed against my skin.

And I reached for yarn.

The Most Special Basket was within grasp, of course, since it's the prettiest one. Almost at random, I grabbed the mink I'd bought in Iceland and a size three needle. I printed out a simple shawl pattern called Shaelyn that I'd already made twice. I didn't want to have to think.

My goal was simple survival.

On the plane, I was upgraded to business class, something that had never happened to me before. My first thought was *Free booze!* The tension of waving away the free drinks, combined with the fear of being alone in a drinking country, gave me a migraine. When I landed in Barcelona, the migraine was the size of the Eurasian landmass and twice as heavy—I could barely walk and ironically, it wasn't from overindulgence.

The taxi got me to my hotel, but I needed food to

protect my stomach from my medication, so I wobbled to a restaurant where I was seated next to the waiters' sangria refilling station, or as I immediately renamed it, Hell. The waiters poured the wine into vast pitchers. They gossiped and poured and then poured some more, carrying each glistening pitcher to a table that wasn't mine. The fruit inside the sangria gleamed—the orange peels shimmering a deep red, the chopped apples winking at me. Drinking, of course, would have made my migraine worse, but that had never stopped me before. In the past, I'd frequently drunk myself into a deeper and worse migraine, all the while insisting that it might help this time.

At the table, I gritted my teeth through the pain, both physical and mental, and managed to order a paella, hoping it would help a little. I held up my hand to block the sangria station from sight, but immediately lowered it, feeling like a complete idiot. Wine wasn't the *sun*—it wouldn't burn me to a crisp.

Or would it?

Tapping desperately at my phone, I emailed a friend I knew was in recovery, telling her my news that I now had nine days sober (somehow I'd gotten another day on my teetotal and agonizing flight), and to my absolute delight, she emailed back within minutes. She said, *BABE! BABE! 9 DAYS SOBER!!!! I promise you it gets better. And if you need/want a queer sober fairy godmother, I WILL BE YOUR QUEER SOBER FAIRY GODMOTHER!*

She was truly the only reason I didn't give up that night and order a glass of red sangria relief. If I hadn't reached out, if she hadn't responded—well, what was nine days sober really? I could just do it again, right?

No.

That was the thing. I didn't think I could. Gritting my teeth through those first eight days had been awful, and now I was in hell. I didn't think I would find the strength to go through the process again.

So the next morning, I had only one mission: to get to a meeting.

The closest one was just a ten-minute walk away, up three flights of stairs. My head pounded as I climbed, the leftover migraine acting like a hangover, which was beyond impolite. No one should go through that kind of pain unless they've done seriously regrettable things the night before.

I sat in one of the folding chairs. My limbs shook. No one seemed to mind when I got out my yarn and cast on the required two stitches for the start of the shawl.

It was a speaker meeting, which meant that one person would speak for about twenty minutes, and then the rest of us could share if we wanted to. The speaker talked about how he was always about *more*. "When I was a kid, I was the one sneaking back to the candy bowl. All the other kids seemed to do okay with a couple of pieces. Me, once that sugar button lit up, I couldn't get enough."

I stared at him, my needles still in my hands. I'd never seen this guy before and never would again, but he was speaking my language. *More versus enough.* The former was what my blood was made of, and I'd never understood the latter. If I liked something (yarn, Cadbury Creme Eggs, whiskey), I would take more, more, *MORE* until I physically couldn't hold or do or endure any more of whatever it was, until I made myself sick or broke or both.

My fingers moved faster as the pattern came back to me. By the time the hour-long meeting was up, the baby shawl was already starting to look like fabric.

The group invited me to go across the pedestrian street to a cafe. Somehow, I managed to nod and walk with them. As they chattered, I knitted and listened. One of them told me about a meeting happening that night in another part of town.

Right there, right then, I decided that my ten days alone in Barcelona would be a sober tour of the city, powered by my clicking needles. At the end of those ten days, my wife would arrive for a week, which was all the time she could take off work. Until then, I'd lean on the meetings and on my needles.

I went to five different locations, attending at least one meeting a day, but often two or even three. I made real friends that I saw day after day, both tourists like me and expats in residence. While in each meeting, I knitted without ceasing. The only times my fingers stopped moving were when we reached into our pockets to pull out one- or two-euro coins for the donation basket that went to the rent of the various rooms. But otherwise, my fingers flashed, even during the Serenity Prayer. As everyone else's eyes closed, I kept my eyes on the mink, on those exact shades of the woolly moss that protected Iceland's lava landscape.

Iceland had played another part in my getting sober, I realized, as I sat in a meeting near the Plaça d'Espanya. In Duty Free on our way home, we'd bought several tiny airplane bottles of Icelandic liqueurs we'd thought might make good gifts, spirits flavored with Icelandic birch bark handpicked in the spring. Handpicked! How cottagecore! How delightful! How twee! Friends would love a thoughtful gift like these little bottles.

On one of my final nights of drinking, I'd stood in the kitchen, frantic. We were out of wine. Lala had the flu and couldn't pop out to the store to buy me more, which, because she hadn't known about my problem, she'd never minded doing for me. I'd felt jangled and wired for hours, so I'd smoked some weed, which meant I couldn't drive, either.

I pawed through our "bar," which was mostly the dregs of unpleasant things I hadn't already come up with an excuse to drink: coffee-flavored bitters that had expired six years before and an applejack whiskey that tasted like socks smelled and had thickened in a disgusting, green way.

And there were those Icelandic airplane bottles.

I drank them, not even taking the time to fully taste them. I needed what I thought they'd give me: relief.

They didn't. I didn't even get the tiniest hint of a buzz. I crawled into bed with my sick wife, wishing I could be her, fighting a simple bug instead of the scorched-soul devastation that made me want to—what? Not die, exactly. I never considered killing myself.

But I didn't want to be alive anymore, not if it meant feeling the way I did.

In the Barcelona meetings with the green-yellow mossy yarn moving through my fingers, I felt air—cold and sweet —fill my lungs. The tension my body always carried started to loosen the more I knitted, the more I walked through the city streets, the more meetings I went to.

I started feeling grateful for small things. The way my feet felt through my shoes' thin soles as I trod over cobblestones. How it felt to wake up without a headache or a murky, all-encompassing sense of existential dread. The way when I scrolled through my phone in the morning, I wasn't worried about ill-conceived late-night texts or tweets or emails.

The first time I heard the Ninth Step Promises in a meeting, I gasped. *We are going to know a new freedom and a new happiness. We will not regret the past nor wish to shut the door on it. We will comprehend the word Serenity and we will know peace.*

The full text promised that I would be amazed before I was halfway through the process. Shoot, I was only twelve days in, and I was already astounded.

In my fingers, the yarn started feeling even softer. I couldn't stop admiring the lace I was making. I smoothed it over my lap and held it up to the light surreptitiously, pretending I was checking a stitch, but really just sitting in awe of how much it had grown in less than two weeks.

Of course, even with a meeting or three every day, most of my alone time in Barcelona was spent *not* being in meetings. One afternoon, I sat in a square enjoying a bottle of Vichy Catalan, the salty mineral water that I couldn't get enough of. I'd ordered a small pizza to eat in the sun. My project bag sat on the table, like it always did. As a woman began to sing in Spanish, her voice filling the plaza, I reached for the bag, intending to knit as I waited for my food.

But when my fingers touched the fiber, I drew back.

This was my recovery shawl now. Every row symbolized time I'd spent with other people who felt the way I did. Every stitch was a prayer, which was a strange, new thing for me. As I've mentioned, I'm not one for prayer, and the one thing that kept turning me off about the meetings was the whole God thing. They kept talking about him, and I kept refusing to listen to that part of it.

But one afternoon, I was with a new friend.

We'd done a few errands, and we were now walking through narrow streets. I struggled to match her stride.

"So, how's it going, the not-drinking?"

I confessed, "It's hard as hell. I'm struggling."

"Have you tried praying?"

"Hell, no."

"Try it."

I was mildly disappointed. Ines *seemed* normal. She hadn't come across as a God freak. I instantly regretted that I'd already agreed to go to a buffet restaurant with her after her phone errand.

"No, thanks."

She shrugged easily and tossed a receipt into a trash can. "What have you got to lose? You're feeling fucked up by not drinking. Just ask for help. See what happens. You don't have to believe in anything. That part doesn't matter."

I dodged a mother dragging two screaming children behind her. "It doesn't matter? I'm just supposed to pray to something I believe doesn't exist?"

"If you don't believe in it, why the hell wouldn't you? It can't hurt you, right? If you don't believe in it?"

She had a point. I'd lick a bathroom doorknob if it might help. I'd pretend to have wings in public and flap like a bird if someone said it would relieve the constant craving. I was crawling out of my skin every night as I walked alone through the Gothic Quarter, bottles of wine flirting with me from restaurant windows, promising their sour relief.

I said, "Do I have to get on my knees? Because no way in hell. I'm not kneeling." Patriarchal bullshit. I wasn't praying to a white man with a beard.

She tossed a smile at me. "That's the way I do it. Do what you want."

This woman was cool. She wore a black leather jacket and had piercings in places most people didn't. She spoke six languages fluently and swore in four more.

But she got on her knees to pray. It didn't make any sense to me.

That night, though, I felt as if I was coming apart at the seams. I'd been sober less than two weeks. I was alone, and I *really* liked drinking alone. It was my favorite way to drink, honestly.

No one would know.

I felt headachy, like I was coming down with the flu, hot and then cold. But I knew it was just this soul-consuming need, this thing I couldn't turn off.

I was desperate.

So, in my rented apartment, I closed the curtains out of shame. No one could see me do this.

I knelt on the red rug. I shut my eyes and folded my hands.

I muttered, "Please help?"

And even though I feel so awkward admitting this, I'm still going to say it: the feeling of needing to drink went away. That very instant.

I rocked back on my heels, falling to a side-sitting position on the floor. My eyes flew open. "What the hell?"

It was as if the need had been lifted out of my chest, stripped away like it had been surgically removed.

I looked for the urge in my mind, like I would prod a sore tooth with my tongue.

I imagined a crisp glass of Chardonnay. A snifter of Laphroaig. A shot of mescal.

The need was gone.

So I gasped, "Thanks."

That was my prayer for the rest of my time in Barcelona. Every morning, I said, "Please help?" At night, I said, "Thanks."

That's all.

It worked.

I waited for the urge to come back. Occasional ravings have come back since, yes, of course. I'm human. But the overwhelming tidal wave of urge, the one I couldn't control, was just. . . gone. Three years later, it has never come back.

Don't worry. I'm not going to try to convert you. I couldn't anyway. I *still* don't believe in God. When people talk about "Him" in meetings, I roll my eyes. Even the words "higher power" kind of make me itch. But that night in my Barcelona Airbnb, I reached out and something reached back. Even if I vaguely think about it as the Universe, I'll never be able to explain it. I don't have to. It worked, that's all.

So as I waited for my pizza at the plaza table as the soprano sang in the open air, I decided not to knit. This shawl was for prayer. Every knit stitch a tiny *help*. Every purl stitch a wee little *thanks*. I'd keep it that way, only knitting in meetings. As the woman sung around the square and passed around a hat into which I dropped two euros, I noticed that I wasn't at all bothered by the drinks on almost every other table around me. I had my salty water, and it was delicious. I felt quenched, in a full and deep way.

My wife arrived, and we traipsed around the city together for a week. Once a day, every day, I popped out to see my friends at a meeting somewhere in town. I became an expert at the Metro and the TMB busses. Lala was impressed with how many parts of town I already knew. "Oh, there's a great cafe just down that alley." Or "I love the bookstore just over there, want to check it out?" We did the tourist things together, the things I'd saved to do with her: Park Guell, a bike tour, and the Picasso museum. We went to La Sagrada Familia, and to my wife's great surprise, I entered the "For Prayer Only" section. I felt like an imposter, but I said in my mind, *Please*. I felt a sweet relief. So I said, *Thank you.*

And we ate—of course, we ate. With my blessing, Lala ordered sangria. She offered not to, because she's not a jerk. She didn't have a drinking problem, so she didn't mind not drinking, a fact which blew my still-drying-out mind. I wanted her to enjoy her time, and to enjoy her drinks, just as I was actually enjoying not drinking.

My mind was clear. For the first time since I could remember, Lala and I talked over dinner, and my attention was fully on her. On us. On the dinner in front of us. There wasn't a running dialogue in the back of my brain that worried, *Am I feeling tipsy? Am I acting drunk? I've had two-*

and-a-half drinks. Can I get another one? Maybe two? When can I order the next one? What should I blame it on? My aching feet from climbing all those stairs at the church? Did I just slur that last word? Should I preemptively mention I'm really tired?

That worried voice was gone. I could focus.

I could connect, which was something I'd always thought wine helped me do. Instead, it had been what kept me apart. Who can listen over that kind of background noise? When the voice stopped nattering, I could hear my wife as clearly as I heard the city bells toll.

The shawl was always within arm's reach, and just touching it for a moment made me feel strong.

When we got home to California, I kept working on it in my favorite early morning meeting, the one where I quickly learned everyone's name, where I was rapidly embraced as someone who was expected to attend. People texted me when I didn't come, just to check on me. One morning, I forgot my project bag, and multiple people asked me where my knitting was. *I like to watch you knit. It's soothing.* My knitting was at home. I'd remember to bring it the next day. But my collected prayers, the pleases and thanks sent out to something I never had to believe in or understand—those were still with me, I found. Even without my knitting in my hands, I could sit back in the meeting and listen with my whole heart.

I eventually finished the shawl. I bound it off in a meeting, of course. It's my most-worn object now, one of my favorite possessions. Knotted at my throat, it's a perfect block against a cold wind and a balm on a difficult day. The fiber has haloed softly, but the stitch definition is still clear.

I still keep my AA chip close by, now on my key ring. I go to fewer meetings than I did in the beginning, but I'm grateful that I'll always be a member. And I always, always, have a knitting project on the go that's only for working on in meetings. The people I give socks to have no idea that the reason their feet are so warm is that each stitch is made with gratitude, that each stitch has a tiny bit of the energy of the people in the rooms.

Iceland helped get me sober. Barcelona helped keep me that way. I got my two-month chip at a meeting in Venice. The most precious of my chips come from a guy named Bob in Oakland at my home group who always reminds me that the twenty-four-hour chip is the most important one of all. One day at a time is a total twelve-step cliché, yes. But clichés come into being because they're obviously true, because they work.

Now, it's just one stitch at a time. One stitch, one breath, one word, each following the other. It's how a life gets made.

EPILOGUE

When the rights for this book reverted to me, I jumped at the chance to publish an updated edition. This time, I get to release the audiobook, which I'd begged my publisher to do (seriously, I did everything but walk on my hands while juggling fire with my feet, trying to get them to understand how knitters and crafters *love* audiobooks). So I've spent hours locked in a recording studio, finally speaking aloud these words to make the audiobook to go along with this edition, and when I say recording studio, I actually mean the bedroom closet of an almost empty house that I lined with moving blankets to dampen the echo.

Why's the house almost empty?

As I've mentioned in the updates, we're in the middle of leaving the country. By the time you read this, due to the time-bending properties of literature, we will have already taken the long-ass plane ride to the other country of my dual citizenship—New Zealand.

Sitting here in the past, in the shell of our house that

holds only the staged furniture for the sale, I'm not sure what we're doing or where we're living when you read this. Perhaps we've settled into an apartment in Wellington and we walk along the wharf every day. Maybe we've bought a house in Christchurch, and I'm swimming regularly in the ocean. Maybe we haven't even stayed! Maybe it went badly and we moved to Bali, instead, or to San Miguel de Allende.

I'm *such* a planner. I like to know what I'm going to eat tomorrow, and what I'm going to knit next. This move has thrown everything up into the air. We have one more week in this staged, sold house before the new owners take the keys. After that? We'll be living out of two suitcases each for the unknowable future, moving from city to city until we fall in love with one. I'm working on getting used to operating with less certainty than I'd like. And ooooh, that's difficult for me.

Know what else is difficult?

Being an *idiot*.

Let me explain. For this international move, we emptied the beloved house we've lived in for fifteen years. The average American home holds 300,000 items, but most of them don't have a Lala kind of collector living in them, so we probably had even more.

We got rid of about 95% of what we owned. We sold things on Craigslist. I took at least twenty car loads to the thrift store, and we had the junk haulers come *three times.* We're definitely people who use things until they wear out. When *we* were done with the couch we got thirdhand on Craigslist ten years ago, I could be sure that no one else would have wanted it.

We're down to two suitcases each for the trip, and we're shipping sixty-seven small book boxes to New Zealand, the majority of them filled with the books they were made to hold. We kept some important things like our favorite mixing bowls and photo albums and my spinning wheel and musical instruments and some artwork, but most of everything else? Gone.

What about the yarn, Rachael?

Such a good question.

In the past ten years, I've had two big fits of minimalism. They come over me like the flu, and I burn with them until I work the fever out of my body. One was when Marie Kondo's book came out, *The Life-Changing Magic of Tidying Up*, and the other was during the early days of the Covid-19 pandemic, when *The Home Edit* was a popular television show. Why, yes, I did organize my books by color, and I thought it was dumb too, until I tried it, and I have to tell you, it's gorgeous.

I didn't get rid of all the yarn, don't worry. I could never do that. And I shouldn't call it minimalism; I should really call it curation. I loved what Ingrid Fetell Lee said about the Kondo craze in *Joyful: The Surprising Power of Ordinary Things to Create Extraordinary Happiness*:

"What I realized is that Kondo's philosophy isn't really minimalism. It's sanity. After all, we still have plenty of stuff. And now that we can see the things we have, our place actually feels more abundant, not less. That's because abundance isn't about just accumulating things. It's about surrounding yourself with a rich palette of textures that enliven your senses. If true minimalism is like clear-cutting a field, Kondo's method is like weeding a garden. It's a process of removing the background noise to create a canvas on which to build a joyful home. Yet it's also worth remembering that just weeding alone doesn't create a beautiful garden. You have to plant flowers, too."

I weeded the *hell* out of my yarn garden, and both times I was left with only what I loved, an absolutely wonderful feeling. I still had yarn, and I had the ability to get (or make) more if I needed to, but all those balls I didn't know what to do with? They were given to the East Bay Depot for Creative Reuse, a crafting thrift store where I'd picked up plenty of inexpensive yarn myself when I was a broke grad student.

We decided to move to New Zealand less than a year after my pandemic cull, meaning there was little time to acquire much extra, but some *had* snuck in, probably from burglars. Burglars are always leaving yarn in my home. Yours, too? They're so weird that way.

So when I got ready to pack the yarn that was coming with us, I had a stern talk with myself. I had to *love* it. You know, of course, that's not enough. I love most of it! It also had to be earmarked for something specific, something I desperately wanted to make. The Lettlopi I'd bought at Álafoss in Iceland was gorgeous, but did I need a Lopa-peysa sweater? I did not. Even in New Zealand at the bottom of the South Island, a relative stone's throw from Antarctica, I'd probably never get chilly enough to need one. I donated those kinds of projects.

After the new culling, I was left with nine or ten projects to pack and send to New Zealand. Yes, I know it's the land of sheep, but yarn is actually quite expensive there, so it (kind of) makes sense, right?

Then I stared at the thirty or forty balls of random, perfect yarn I didn't know what to do with. Some of the skeins had been in my stash for twenty years now, having made it through every other culling.

I sat cross-legged in front of them, and we had the talk.

"Right, then. I'm very sorry to be the bearer of bad news, but you all have to go."

A faint scream rose from the collection.

"I'm serious. We've been together a long time now, but we've never been inspired to *do* anything together. Don't you think that's telling? Wouldn't we be better off going our separate ways?"

The screaming got louder and more piercing.

I shook my head. "I'm sorry, but I've decided. I'm one hundred percent positive I'm making the right decision."

As I piled them into a garbage bag—the indignity!—one bit me and another punched my knuckles.

Only one spoke, a breathy voice I almost missed hearing. *"But for packing..."*

"What?"

"We're useful..."

O FRABJOUS DAY!

I'd actually been considering buying packing material! But right here, right in front of me, was the perfect packing material.

I kept putting the yarn into the bag, but this time I promised each ball it was going on an adventure across the ocean on a container ship, and most of them were thrilled. A couple of them still sulked, but that's angora for you.

That's why, on the master manifest that we'll present to the shipping company, each box listed says something like,

"Fiestaware dishes, random yarn." Or "Photo album, year-books, random yarn." Random Yarn should be my next band name, and I'm telling you, *nothing* is better packing material than balls and skeins of lovely, fluffy yarn.

Oh, but I was also telling you about The Idiot, who is me.

So I packed and packed and packed some more. Very carefully, and with incredible foresight, I kept out four small projects that would keep me company. I chose one intricate lace shawl pattern, a simple scarf, and two sock projects. Perfect, right? That would keep me busy for months, until either our boxes arrived or I caved and bought new New Zealand yarn.

Then, on the last panicked day, hours before the new floors went into our house, meaning we had to be *all* the way out for a few days, *I accidentally packed all my projects.*

What did this lead to? A crisis? A meltdown? Yes! Did it spur me to spend a full day planning how I'd learn to tat? Yes, indeed. I wanted a tatted choker—so adorably goth! Instead of paying $15 for one on Etsy, I'd just learn an entirely new fiber craft.

Then, for about seven hours, I obsessed over a new plan to hand-sew my own all-linen clothing from a pattern I'd draft myself (because of course, I gave away my sewing machine). I imagined myself hand-sewing steady seams, my eyes as calm as the linen under my fingers.

But then, of course, I came to my senses. I drove to the nearest yarn shop, bought some red wool and a size three needle and cast on for a cowl called Starshower. As soon as the stitches started slipping through my fingers, I was home again. My heart rate lowered.

With yarn in my hands, I know who I am, even if I'm not sure where we're going.

Now, I keep imagining myself on the other side of the world, seven thousand miles away, finally in a home we've agreed to stay in for a while. With a razor blade, I slice at the tape I put on while standing in our old house. I pull out books that I love or haven't yet read and put them on the bookshelf that I can't quite picture in a room I haven't yet seen. I'm tired from unpacking, and a little overwhelmed. I'm fighting tears of sorrow and of joy, and it just feels like a *lot*.

Then, in a spot between two odd-sized books, a skein of glorious purple and red jumps into my hands. I remember buying it in a little store in Maryland with my sister at my side. I hadn't needed it then—it was just gorgeous and so achingly soft, and I'd bought it impulsively. How could I have known I'd need it *now*? How could I have ever guessed that I'd bought it for this very moment, when it fills my hands and soothes the pain I feel in my lower jaw where I've been gritting my teeth together for hours?

Yarn isn't a substitute for family or friends, I know that.

But it is a balm, isn't it?

Yarn leads us back to ourselves.

Yarn, I'm hoping, will also lead me to my next group of friends. When I worry about meeting new people in our new country, I remember this: somewhere, very close to wherever we land, there will be a knitting circle. I'll go to it, gripping my knitting with sweaty, nervous fingers.

But the one thing I've learned from getting rid of things over the years, is that when you make room for something, the something comes. These new-to-me knitters will open the circle to me with smiles.

Somewhere in those ranks, I'll find new beloved friends. They'll never replace my old ones, of course. I'm just making room for more, the same way you, as a crafter, occasionally make room for more stash, or books, or whatever it is that you love best. Speaking of books, thanks for making room for *this* book, for being with me here, in these pages. We're now connected, you and I, and I'm so grateful for that.

Onward!

HOTTIE KNITTING PATTERN

Yarnagogo's Easy Cabled Hot-Water Bottle Cozy

Just right for trying cables for the first time!

Go to rachaelherron.com/hottie to see pics and for the free Ravelry PDF pattern!

Finished Measurements
    Circumference: 17 inches
    Length: 18 inches

You Will Need
    200 yards worsted weight yarn
    1 US size 7 (4.5 mm) 16-inch circular, or size to achieve gauge
    Stitch markers
    Cable needle
    Yarn needle

Gauge

16 sts and 24 rounds = 4 inches in Stockinette stitch

Directions

Cast on 52 sts and join to work in the round. Place a marker at beginning of round and after 26 sts to mark sides.

Round 1: *K1f&b, knit to 1 st before marker, k1f&b, slip marker; repeat from * once—4 sts increased.

Rounds 2–4: Repeat Round 1—68 sts at end of Round 4.

Rounds 5–9: K12, p2, k6, p2, k12, slip marker, k34.

Round 10: K12, p2, slip the next 3 sts onto cable needle and hold behind work, knit the next 3 sts from the left-hand needle, then knit the 3 sts from the cable needle, p2, knit to end of round.

Repeat Rounds 5–10 until piece measures 10 inches from beginning.

Neck

Decrease Round: *K1, ssk, work to 3 sts before marker, k2tog, k1, slip marker; repeat from * once—4 sts decreased.

Maintaining cable pattern, repeat Decrease Round three more times—52 sts remain.

Ribbing Round: *K2, p2; repeat from * to end of round for rib.

Repeat this round until the neck is 8 inches long (total length is 18 inches). Bind off all sts loosely in rib.

Finishing

Using yarn needle, sew bottom closed. Weave in ends. Roll hot-water bottle so it slips into the neck, and you're good to go! Enjoy the warmth.

List of Abbreviations

K—Knit

K1f&b—Knit one front and back (increase 1 stitch)

K2tog—Knit two together (decrease 1 stitch)

P—Purl

Ssk—Slip two stitches, one at a time, as if to knit to right-hand needle, return these two stitches to left-hand needle in turned position, and knit them together through the back loops (decrease 1 stitch)

St(s)—Stitch(es)

Stockinette stitch—in the round, knit every round

ABOUT RACHAEL

Official Biography:

(It's kind of funny to include a bio when we've just spent so much time together, isn't it? But here you go.)

Rachael Herron is the internationally bestselling author of more than two dozen books, including thriller (under R.H. Herron), mainstream fiction, feminist romance, memoir, and nonfiction about writing. She received her MFA in writing from Mills College, Oakland, and she teaches writing extension workshops at both UC Berkeley and Stanford. She is a proud member of the NaNoWriMo Writer's Board. She's a New Zealand citizen as well as an American and is currently living in Aotearoa.

She *loves* to hear from readers! (Really.) Please hit her up at https://instagram.com/rachaelherron or https://twitter.com/RachaelHerron, or email her at rachael@rachaelherron.com.

And if you liked this book, the absolutely best thing

you could do for Rachael would be to leave it a review!
Thank you in advance — it really helps!

And if you like her voice, get some more of it in your email inbox? (She writes emails like she writes these essays.)

For readers: https://rachaelherron.com/subscribe/

For writers: https://rachaelherron.com/write/

Made in the USA
Columbia, SC
16 July 2022